Networks in a Flash

Making Broadband Work for You

Networks in a Flash
Making Broadband Work for You

Hrair Aldermeshian
Thomas B. London

SP SILICON PRESS
Summit, NJ 07901, USA
www.silicon-press.com

Networks in a Flash: Making Broadband Work for You
© 2003 by HRATOM LLC

Silicon Press
25 Beverly Road
Summit, NJ 07901
USA

First Edition
Printing 9 8 7 6 5 4 3 2 1   Year 07 06 05 04 03

Cover design: Shelley Beckler Modi
Printed on acid-free paper

Library of Congress Cataloging-in-Publication Data

Aldermeshian, Hrair
    Networks in a Flash: Making Broadband Work for You/
    Hrair Aldermeshian, Thomas B. London. – First edition
        p. cm.
    Includes index.
    ISBN 0-929306-25-2
    1. Wireless LANs. 2. Digital subscriber lines. 3. Broadband communication
    systems. 4. Ethernet (Local area network system). I. London, Thomas B., II. Title.
TK5105.78.A43 2003
    004.6'8--dc21   2002012444

*To Adrienne and Elaine, and Danica, Jeremy, Laura, and Peter.
Their love and support makes all things possible. Their
willingness to test and use new technology helped initiate this
book. Their frustration with network features that "don't work"
encouraged us onward.*

Table of Contents

Preface

Congratulations! If you are reading this book, you are contemplating creating a network of home or office computers, and connecting it to the Internet through a high-speed, always connected **broadband** service. Today most of you have a choice of broadband service including broadband cable, typically offered by your local cable TV provider, or broadband DSL  (Digital Subscriber Line), typically offered by your phone company. We show you how to connect your computers to the Internet quickly and directly, using recipes that are straightforward, recommendations that reduce your overall cost, and blueprints that increase your security and "Web safety."

After working in the communications industry for decades building global networks that supported large numbers of consumers and corporations, the difficulties we encountered when we built our own home and office networks surprised us. We thought that others could benefit from a simple, easy-to-follow "how to" book describing the shortest path to a functioning and secure network. We have tried to create that book.

Throughout this book, we strive to present just the right amount of detail to allow assembly, installation, and operations by people not specially trained in computer networking, computers, or computer hardware. We illustrate the details by showing one example that works. Given the choice, we always choose to present the simplest explanations and instructions that will suffice. We provide a complete picture, so we have included most of the additional details, jargon, and complex explanations near the end of the book.

Our goal is to provide you with the shortest path to a connected, secure, and functional home or office network. Once you have set up your network, you can delve into detail as needed by reading or re-reading the material included in this book.

 Our aim is to make this book a complete and easy guide to getting your home or office network connected to the Internet. The book includes complete details, correct and easy steps to follow, and a good set of recommendations. You should not be left adrift if you follow the instructions included here.

However, sometimes all of us need more support than can be gleaned from a static book. To that end, we have linked the contents of this book with a website, `www.BooksInAFlash.com`, containing updated content, support tools, and services. As the industry introduces new products, services, and technologies, we will keep the information and recommendations on the website current and up-to-date.

There are many reasons to network your home and office computers. When your computers form a network, they can easily share one broadband Internet connection. All your computers can connect to the Internet at the same time on the same broadband connection. In addition, one connection to the Internet gives you a single point to protect your computers from intruders and mischief. Finally, once networked, the computers can interact and share printers, files, peripherals, and disk space.

This book describes how you can network your computers using either wired or wireless Ethernet technology. Using wires has the advantage of low cost, and high reliability, but may present installation challenges. Using wireless technology has the advantage of ease of installation and mobility, but may be a little more costly and a little more difficult to configure in order to preserve security. We provide details that help you make an informed and appropriate choice. In either case, we also show you how to configure the elements to maintain privacy, safety, and security.

The scope of this book

This book includes material that helps you understand how the Internet works, material that helps you create and install your home or office network, and material that helps you troubleshoot and operate your network. Some of the material may already be familiar to you, while some of the material may be too detailed. That is OK. We have structured the book for a broad audience: from novices to networking gurus. Each should find what is needed to get their network and broadband access up and running.

 To help you find the most effective path through the book, we describe several "roadmaps" to provide each reader a guide to the most direct and easy path to a functional and secure network.

The examples and detailed instructions included in this book describe the latest versions of Windows™-based computers, network components, and virus protection software from popular manufacturers. Including details about each version and each manufacturer would make this book too long and difficult to read. We believe, however, that readers should have little difficulty completing the installation, since the overall approach should be the same, and any differences should be minor. We intend to include a more comprehensive list of detailed instructions describing each variation on our website, as we describe later.

We include instructions on the most popular versions of the Windows Operating System: Windows XP™, Windows 2000™, Windows ME™, and Windows 98™. Readers using older versions of Windows or other operating systems may find more details on our website.

Notations and symbols used in this book

In many places in the book, we refer to websites or to information located on websites. You can recognize those references when you see text formatted thusly:

    www.booksInAFlash.com/index.html

You should be able to retrieve the information by entering the referenced text in your web browser.

Quite often, we provide instructions guiding you through a sequence of steps on your computer. In some of these situations, you need to maneuver through a sequence of menus. For example, we show such a sequence in the following way:

Select **Start→Settings→Control Panel**

This means first select the **Start** menu (from the bottom left side of your Windows' desktop), next select the **Settings** entry, and finally select the **Control Panel** entry. The following figure shows the result of this sequence.

Sometimes, we provide different sequences for different versions of Windows Operating System. If your computer is running Windows XP, we assume you are using the new Windows XP Start menu interface. The figure below shows the sequence **Start→Control Panel**, that is, select **Start** and then select **Control Panel**. (If you have chosen to use the "Windows Classic" Start menu interface, your start menu looks like the one shown previously. The instructions we give for Windows 2000 will closely match the steps you will need to take. We intend to include a more comprehensive list of detailed instructions describing each variation on our website, as we describe later.)

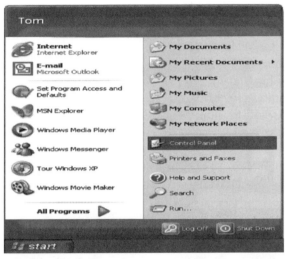

During the installation procedures, a window may often pop up into which you must enter information or where you must do something to continue the activity. For example, given the entry window of the following figure, we instruct you: "Enter the **Computer description** and **Computer name** and click **Next**."

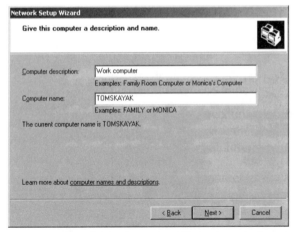

Sometimes, you see a small black arrow, ▼, in the window that indicates a choice. We instruct you to choose a specific entry from the drop-down menu, that is, you need to click on the black arrow to display the drop-down menu and select the appropriate choice. In most instances, some fields within the window will change by that action.

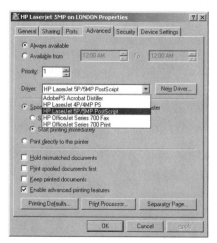

 In a number of instances, we have marked some steps where you need to exercise special care, for example, where you need to enter your own computer name (not the name given in the example in the book). Wherever you see the "exclamation mark" shown at the left, be sure to take special care in reading and following the instructions.

Finally, we include at the end of some chapters a table that acts as a roadmap to "what you should read next." The table lets you know what chapters you can safely skip to streamline completing the installation of your network. If you do not see this table at the end of a chapter, you should continue reading the next chapter.

If you are	Read next
Someone wanting it "done for them"	
A novice	
A typical user	
A power user	

Acknowledgements

The authors would like to acknowledge and thank all who supported the creation of this book, especially our reviewers, whose efforts greatly improved the book. In particular, we would like to thank John A. Newell for his meticulous and thorough comments and numerous suggestions. Greg D. Buzzard and Patricia L. Harris carefully read the manuscript and gave many helpful recommendations. All remaining errors and inadequacies are due solely to the authors.

Narain Gehani and Silicon Press, Inc. provided substantial review comments and consistently good counsel. Shelley Beckler Modi created the cover design and greatly improved the appearance of the book.

Most importantly, our families, especially Adrienne and Elaine, endured, supported, nurtured, reviewed, and sustained us through the long days, long phone calls, early mornings, and late evenings. The authors cannot imagine writing this book without them.

Introduction

1-1   The need for home and office networks

In this chapter, we review why home and office networks are important, and how to use this book to get your network up and running quickly. In subsequent chapters, we introduce the general area of networking, the Internet, and all that. With this information, you will find it easy to set up your network.

Why install and maintain a network in your home or office? Although there are many answers, the two main reasons usually center on the need for the computers in your home or office to communicate with each other to share resources, and to connect your computers to the Internet with efficiency, safety, and security.

There is beauty and magic in the technology developed to support the Internet and the World Wide Web (WWW). Currently available hardware and software connect computers and servers together in standard and agreed ways (called **protocols**). This technology is now available in inexpensive and easy-to-use packaging to connect the computers in your home or office with each other, and to connect them to the big Internet.

In this book, we use the term **mini-internet** to refer to the collection of computers, printers and other computer devices in your home or office network. You can manage mini-internets and make them secure, and they easily connect to the big Internet through a single high-speed and shared connection. In the future, mini-internets will support voice, data, and video services.

Most computers now come with the features (hardware and software) you need to network them. In fact, you will see that once so connected, they can support a host of other useful and desirable capabilities including the sharing of data, files, and printers. In later chapters, we show you exactly what you need to do. For now, let us review why you are doing this.

By creating a mini-internet in your home or office, you can:

1. Share a single broadband connection to the Internet

2. Connect multiple computers, allowing them to talk to each other to

    • Play games, collaborate on documents and presentations

    • Share printers, scanners and other peripherals

    • Share files, documents and disk space

3. Define a single security point for protecting all the home or office computers from intrusions and mischief

4. Continue to use your older computers and peripherals as you install and begin to use newer ones

    • Once networked, the older, "experienced" machines should continue providing value with little or no additional investment and effort

    • The older computer can backup the newer one in case of a hardware or software failure

1-2   *Wired, wireless and all that*

You have two ways to connect your home or office computers together: you can choose either wired or wireless "connections."

Using wires or cables to connect network elements together has the advantage of low cost, reliability, performance, and ease of configuration. Its main disadvantage lies with the cost and difficulty in laying the cables. Running cables in a room or between two adjacent rooms can be quick and easy, but running cables between distant rooms or between floors can be difficult for the novice installer. In addition, they can be unsightly and unsafe.

Wireless networks for the home or office have the advantage of quick and easy installation, mobility for laptops, and easy growth (you can add another computer to your network without worrying about the location of cables or other computers). However, wireless components are more costly, more difficult to configure, and can be less reliable (their performance can change depending on external factors, e.g., radio interference or other wireless users close by). However, there are no unsightly cables to worry about or expensive installation costs. In addition, you can "bring up" a network within minutes.

There is no single "right" answer to the "wired or wireless network" question. There are just too many variations in circumstances to permit a single approach. Therefore, we describe in detail how you can make an informed and appropriate choice. Once you have decided upon the "right" solution for your situation, we give you details and support for either wired or wireless installation. In fact, you may find that a "hybrid" installation with both wired and wireless connections is right for you. If you decide upon a wireless installation, we also show you how to configure the elements to maintain privacy, safety, and security.

1-3   *You're ready to go – how to proceed*

We have provided in this book a wealth of information and detail, but you do not need to read and digest the entire book before you set up your network and start using your mini-internet. The sequence you follow depends on your background, expertise, and requirements. Use the entries in *Table 1-1* to find the next "best" chapter to read.

If you are	Read next
Someone wanting it "done for them"	*Section 1-4*
A novice	*Section 1-5*
A typical user	*Section 1-6*
A power user	*Section 1-7*

Table 1-1: What you should read next!

However, sometimes all of us need more support than can be gleaned from a book. To that end, we have integrated the content of this book with a website, `www.BooksInAFlash.com`, and a set of support tools and services. We believe this will maintain the value of our procedures and recommendations even as the industry introduces new products, services, and technologies.

We partitioned our website into several areas, each addressing the kinds of problems and issues you will encounter when setting up and maintaining your network. Please visit our website and explore the possibilities. We describe the various services available to you in *Chapter 13, Additional Assistance.*

1-4 Roadmap for those who want networks done for them

Congratulations! You have chosen to install and use a broadband network for your home or office. We understand that your primary concern is getting your home or office network up and running quickly and securely. We provide you with concise and direct recipes to accomplish this with a minimum investment in time or resources. We guide
you through all of the steps, and provide just enough background to keep your network running and your business functioning.

In addition to the instruction and assistance given in this book, we also provide links to a network of professional services that can help you plan, order, purchase, install, configure, and maintain your network. You should start your reading in *Chapter 13, Additional Assistance*, where you will find links to professional installers, continuing support for security and virus issues, as well as notification services for updates and upgrades to your network components. You will find the checklist of questions listed in *Appendix A-1* helpful in assessing installation proposals.

Even if you have decided to hire someone to install your network, you should read a few of the chapters in the book to ease dealing with the contractor. Start with the roadmap summary given in *Chapter 2,*

Insanely Quick Roadmap. It gives you a quick high-level overview of the steps needed to get your network up and running. You should then quickly browse through *Chapter 3, Network Concepts* and *Chapter 4, Network Components*, to get a rapid introduction to Internet concepts and the network components you will be dealing with. Don't worry, there will be no quiz given.

You will likely need to participate in the decision to obtain broadband service from a cable or a DSL provider: *Chapter 5, Planning for Broadband Service* walks you through the issues and tradeoffs. You will then be ready to hand off the planning and detailed layout and design of your network. Scanning *Chapter 6, Planning Your Network* helps you understand this process and make the right choices.

At your leisure, you should read *Chapter 7, Setting Up Cable Modem Service*, if you will be using broadband cable service, or in *Chapter 8, Setting Up DSL Modem* if DSL service; *Chapter 9, Setting Up Your Network* and *Chapter 10, Connecting: Put it All Together*. These describe the steps that the installer will need to follow.

To keep the computers in your network protected from viruses and attacks from hackers, you will need to make sure that you have "industrial strength" virus protection running on your computers. *Chapter 11, Securing Your Network* shows you how.

If you intend to set up a mini-internet on your network to share printers or files between your computers, you should read and understand the steps listed in *Chapter 12, Printer and File Sharing*. You should also read at your leisure the remaining chapters. They provide an overview of network security issues and encryption, links to our website for additional support and services, and troubleshooting assistance organized as a sequence of questions and answers.

You should now be prepared! Skip now to *Chapter 13, Additional Assistance,* and then to *Chapter 2, Insanely Quick Roadmap* and start your journey!

1-5   Roadmap for the novice

Congratulations! You have chosen to install and use a broadband network for your home or office. Although this may appear to be a daunting task, you should be comforted by the knowledge that it is indeed easy and doable. We guide you through all of the steps, and provide just enough background for you to consider yourself an experienced network user.

 You should start by reading through the roadmap summary given in *Chapter 2, Insanely Quick Roadmap*. It gives you a quick high-level overview of the steps that you will need to follow. You should then quickly read *Chapter 3, Network Concepts* and *Chapter 4, Network Components* to get a rapid introduction to Internet concepts and the network components you will be dealing with. Don't worry, there will be no quiz given. This information will ease your network installation and operations.

You will next need to decide whether to obtain broadband service from a cable or a DSL provider. *Chapter 5, Planning for Broadband Service* walks you through the issues and tradeoffs. You will then be ready to plan the detailed layout and design of your network. We show you how to create a blueprint indicating where each computer and each network component is to be located, and how you will connect it all together. Reading *Chapter 6, Planning Your Network* helps you complete this task.

Establishing a broadband connection to the Internet is covered in *Chapter 7, Setting Up Cable Modem Service*, if you will be using broadband cable service, or in *Chapter 8, Setting Up DSL Modem* if DSL service. *Chapter 9, Setting Up Your Network* shows you how to complete the installation of the wired or wireless networking elements. You will now be ready to configure the software on each computer.

Chapter 10, Connecting: Put it All Together steps you through the process of configuring your computer and network elements to work together. It shows you how to complete the Windows configuration steps to create your network. This chapter is long and detailed, but that is because we have mapped out each step and contingency in detail. You will only need to follow a fraction of the steps listed there. When you complete these steps, your home or office network will be up and running!

To keep the computers in your network protected from viruses and attacks from hackers, you will need to make sure that you have "industrial strength" virus protection running on your computers. *Chapter 11, Securing Your Network* shows you how.

If you intend to setup a mini-internet on your network to share printers or files between your computers, you will need to read and follow the steps listed in *Chapter 12, Printer and File Sharing*. You should also read the remaining chapters at your leisure. They provide an overview of network security issues and encryption, and troubleshooting assistance organized as a sequence of questions and answers. Finally, in *Chapter 13, Additional Assistance*, we describe how to use our website for additional support and services.

You should now be prepared! Skip now to *Chapter 2, Insanely Quick Roadmap* and start your journey!

1-6   Roadmap for the typical user

Congratulations! You have chosen to install and use a broadband networking for your home or office. You are probably comfortable with using your personal computer to surf the Web and read your email. The task of planning, installing, and operating your own network and mini-internet will build upon these skills, likely adding only a few new ones. We guide you through all of the steps,  providing you with extra detail and assistance when you need it. In addition, in *Chapter 17, Consolidated Troubleshooting* we give you answers to many problems that you may encounter.

You should start by reading through the roadmap summary given in *Chapter 2, Insanely Quick Roadmap*. It gives you a quick high-level overview of the steps that you will need to follow. You can skip *Chapter 3, Network Concepts* and *Chapter 4, Network Components*, or quickly browse to refresh or augment your knowledge of Internet concepts and the network components you will be dealing with. This information will greatly ease your network installation and operations.

You will next need to decide whether you can and should obtain broadband service from a cable or a DSL provider: *Chapter 5, Planning for Broadband Service* walks you through the issues and tradeoffs. You will then be ready to plan the detailed layout and design of your network. We show you how to create a blueprint indicating where each computer and each network component is to be located, and how you will connect it all together. Reading *Chapter 6, Planning Your Network* helps you complete this task.

Establishing a broadband connection to the Internet is covered in *Chapter 7, Setting Up Cable Modem Service*, if you will be using broadband cable service, or in *Chapter 8, Setting Up DSL Modem* if DSL service. *Chapter 9, Setting Up Your Network* shows you how to complete the installation of the wired or wireless networking elements. After this, you will be ready to configure the software on each computer.

Chapter 10, Connecting: Put it All Together steps you through the process of configuring your computer and network elements to work together. It shows you how to complete the Windows configuration steps to create your network. This chapter is long and detailed, but that is because we have mapped out each step and contingency. You will only need to follow a fraction of the steps listed there. When you complete these steps, your home or office network will be up and running!

To keep the computers in your network protected from viruses and attacks from hackers, you will need to make sure that you have "industrial strength" virus protection running on your computers. *Chapter 11, Securing Your Network* shows you how.

If you intend to setup a mini-internet on your network to share printers or files between your computers, you will need to read and follow the steps listed in *Chapter 12, Printer and File Sharing*. You should also read the remaining chapters at your leisure. They provide an overview of network security issues and encryption, and troubleshooting assistance organized as a sequence of questions and answers. Finally, in *Chapter 13, Additional Assistance*, we describe how to use our website for additional support and services.

You should now be prepared! Skip now to *Chapter 2, Insanely Quick Roadmap* and start your journey!

1-7   Roadmap for the power user

Congratulations! You have chosen to install and use a broadband network for your home or office. You should already be familiar with the technical concepts and the needed components, so we can quickly skip to the real meat. We do that, while we provide enough support to help you through any unforeseen troubles.

You should start by reading through the roadmap summary given in *Chapter 2, Insanely Quick Roadmap*. It gives you a quick high-level overview of the steps that you will need to follow.

If you have not already decided on a broadband service provider, you should quickly scan *Chapter 5, Planning for Broadband Service*. You will then be ready to plan the detailed layout and design of your network: we show you how to create a blueprint indicating where each computer and each network component is to be located, and how you will connect it all together. Reading *Chapter 6, Planning Your Network* will help you complete this task.

You should be able to read quickly through *Chapter 7, Setting Up Cable Modem Service* if you will be using broadband cable service, or *Chapter 8, Setting Up DSL Modem* if DSL service. *Chapter 9, Setting Up Your Network* should provide a quick review of completing the installation of the wired or wireless networking elements. At this point, you will be ready to configure the software on each computer on your network.

If you need help configuring the network adapters or the network settings on your router or any of your computers, follow *Chapter 10, Connecting: Put it All Together*. It shows you how to complete the Windows configuration steps to create your network.

If you are not up to date with virus protection, *Chapter 11, Securing Your Network* shows you how to setup and run commercially available virus protection software. We strongly recommend that you guard your network and your computers with industrial-strength virus protection.

Chapter 12, Printer and File Sharing can provide you with any needed pointers on setting up sharing on your mini-internet. *Chapter 14, Protecting your Network*, *Chapter 15, Viruses and Malicious Software*, and *Chapter 16, Encryption and Authentication*, provide an easy basis for understanding security and encryption concepts, important ideas that underlie how the Internet functions. *Chapter 17, Consolidated Troubleshooting* gives you answers to many problems that you may encounter. Finally, *Chapter 13, Additional Assistance* describes how to use our website for additional support and services.

You should now be prepared! Skip now to *Chapter 2, Insanely Quick Roadmap* and start the installation!

What you should read next

If you are	Read next
Someone wanting it "done for them"	*Chapter 13, Additional Assistance*
A novice	*Chapter 2, Insanely Quick Roadmap*
A typical user	*Chapter 2, Insanely Quick Roadmap*
A power user	*Chapter 2, Insanely Quick Roadmap*

2

Insanely Quick Roadmap

In this chapter, we list all the necessary steps for the quick and easy setup of your network and mini-internet. In all instances, we list the chapter or section that provides the details of what you need to do. If you need further assistance, please visit our website: www.BooksInAFlash.com.

1. Contact a cable or DSL provider to plan for service.

    If you do not know how to do this, see *Chapter 5*.

2. Create an inventory of the computers, printers, and similar devices. Include the names of the computers.

    If you do not know how to do this, see *Section 6-1*.

3. Create a layout of your network, and place computer and network resources where you would like them to be. Identify the location where your broadband service will "enter" your home or office.

    If you do not know how to do this, see *Section 6-2*.

4. Decide if you will be creating a wired network, a wireless network, or a network with wired and wireless components.

    If you do not know how to do this, see *Section 6-3*.

5. Create a list of the network components (router, switches, etc.) and cables you will need, based on your network layout and your service provider.

    If you do not know how to do this, see *Section 6-4-1, Section 6-5-1,* or *Section 6-6-1.*

6. Contact a cable or DSL provider to arrange for service.

    If you do not know how to do this, see *Chapter 7* (for cable) or *Chapter 8* (for DSL).

7. Purchase the items on your parts list from a local retailer, or do it via fax or the Web.

    If you do not know how to do this, see *Section 9-1.*

8. After you have all the necessary network components, power off your computers, printers, and cable or DSL modem (if already installed and powered).

    If you do not know how to do this, see *Section 9-2.*

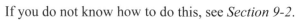

9. Using the above purchased components, build your mini-internet from your computers, printers, cables, network components and cable/DSL modem.

    If you do not know how to do this, see *Section 9-3*, *Section 9-4*, and *Section 9-5.*

10. Power on and configure the network settings for the computer nearest to the modem. We refer to this as the "first" computer.

    If you do not know how to do this, see *Section 10-1.*

11. Power on the router. Start the "first" computer, and configure the router.

If you do not know how to do this, see *Section 10-2*.

12. Power off the router and the computer. Power on the modem. Wait 2 minutes and power on the router.

If you do not know how to do this, see *Section 10-4*.

13. Power on the "first" computer. Test network and Internet access.

If you do not know how to do this, see *Section 10-5*.

14. Power on and configure the network settings of additional computers. Restart computer when complete.

If you do not know how to do this, see *Section 10-6*.

15. For advanced topics, such as setting up virus protection and file and printer sharing, see *Chapters 11 and 12*.

That is it. If you successfully complete these steps, you have created a working and secure network for your home or office.

What you should read next

If you are	Read next
Someone wanting it "done for them"	Quickly browse *Chapter 3, Network Concepts*
A novice	Quickly read *Chapter 3, Network Concepts*
A typical user	Browse or skip *Chapter 3, Network Concepts*
A power user	Quickly scan *Chapter 5, Planning for Broadband Service*

Part 1
Background

3

Network Concepts

3-1   Basics of the Internet

The Internet is really a wonderfully effective way for computers to send messages to each other. When you download a program or a web page, you send a message to the computer that has the program or web page, and you receive messages in return that include the information you requested.

With a fast connection to the Internet, for instance, one using cable or DSL, you typically can send and receive these messages quickly. That is because these connections have a high bandwidth and can transfer quite a lot of information quickly. The term **bandwidth** describes the amount of information delivered in a fixed amount of time.

In the sections below, we describe the basics of the Internet by comparing it to something we all know well: mail and package delivery. This should demystify the concepts so that you will be able to see that installing your computers and network is simple and easy to understand. We describe how packets of information travel through the Internet, how computers have addresses associated with them, how we can address a computer by a name, and how we get help from the Internet to translate names to addresses.

3-1-1   IP (Internet Protocol) addresses

Consider the physical world of letters and packages, homes and businesses, and addresses. **Addresses** are the generally agreed upon descriptive labels of the geographical locations of homes, businesses or things. Before sending a letter or package, we need to know the address of the intended recipient. In order for the recipient to respond or reply, they will need to know the return address.

There is nothing magical happening here: addresses are the way we expedite the delivery of letters and packages.

Some businesses want to advertise their name, and frequently spend a good deal of money to get people to know and use. **Names** are the generally agreed upon descriptive tags or labels for people, businesses or things (again, they actually describe something a bit deeper, but this is all we need now).

We are all familiar with the differences between addresses and names. For example, we are quite comfortable with either "the restaurant at 357 First Street" or "Joe's Diner." Clearly, addresses are more precise and specific, but not always complete or accurate: imagine a situation where Joe's has moved or gone out of business and another restaurant has taken its place. In addition, many people or businesses may reside at the same address.

It would be very convenient if we could use addresses and names interchangeably. However, except for a few exceptions, we cannot send mail and packages directed only to names. Using addresses and names interchangeably is what we want for delivery of messages in the Internet, where computers, services, networks, and companies are moving all the time. The next sections quickly describe how the Internet makes all this work quickly and efficiently.

We started the above discussion by observing that each deliverable location for letters and packages had a recognized address. In the world of Internet networking, the same is true for each computer "connected" to the Internet. It will have a recognized address.

The two characteristics of addresses important to us are uniqueness and "deliverability." The uniqueness guarantees that there is no confusion on how or where to deliver a letter. The "deliverability" ensures that given an address on a letter, it is clear how to route the letter through the system of post offices. Looking at the address tells which should be the next post office to handle the letter (or which mail carrier should carry the letter for final delivery).

Public Internet addresses, called **IP (Internet Protocol) addresses**, have both these characteristics: they are unique and they are deliverable (we explain in a bit that the Internet term is "routable"). So every computer (or computer-like device) on the Internet has a unique and deliverable IP address.

IP addresses all look like four numbers with periods between them: e.g., `192.168.5.100`. Don't worry; you will not need to remember many of these! Of course, there are a few rules about which particular numbers are legitimate to use, such as ranging between 0 and 255. Some addresses are reserved for special uses. We discuss those beginning with `192.168` when we discuss "private" IP addresses. *Table 3-1* gives some examples of valid and invalid IP addresses.

Address	Comment
`192.168.1.1`	Legitimate IP address
`66.77.65.231`	Legitimate IP address
`543.177.3.1`	Invalid IP address: 543 is bigger than 253
`127.101.1`	Invalid IP address: only 3 numbers

Table 3-1: Valid and invalid IP addresses

3-1-2   Static and dynamic IP addresses

Your town or city assigned your home and business address to you. Likewise, your Internet Service Provider (your cable or DSL network provider) assigns IP addresses to you. However, unlike home addresses, service providers frequently provide you with a temporary or "dynamic" IP address. These are normal in every respect; except an IP address assigned to you may change. This is normally not something to be concerned about, except if you want to support an Internet server that provides a service to others. Later on, we discuss the need for permanent IP addresses.

When you set up broadband service, your service provider will tell you whether you have "**static**" (permanent) or "**dynamic**" (temporary) IP addresses. (A bit of techno-babble: if your service provider gives you "dynamic" addresses, then they typically support something called "DHCP", which is the standard way that addresses are given to you). This is something that happens automatically and you do not need to concern yourself with how this works.

3-1-3   Private and public IP addresses

One final twist on IP addresses: in addition to being either static or dynamic, they can also be either "public" or "private." **Public** IP addresses are unique and are **routable** (deliverable): when Internet "post offices" (actually routers and switches) see these addresses on messages, they know which "post office" should forward the messages to ensure delivery. On the other hand, **private** IP addresses may not be unique and are not deliverable. Internet "post offices" have no idea how to handle them. In fact, they just ignore them (equivalent to the "dead letter office").

Typically, Internet service providers (ISPs) or local network administrators will assign IP addresses for your computer. The IP address that you get will be set as static or dynamic, and as either private or public. As a typical user, there is nothing for you to do but note the type of the assigned IP address.

Private IP addresses start with "192.168," so they all look like 192.168.100.1. Since they are not unique, thousands of computers have the IP address of 192.168.0.1.[1]

Computers that do not connect directly to the Internet can use private IP addresses. As an analogy, consider a business with many employees in a large building. Each employee may have an office, each with a unique office number identifying that office within the building. The post office delivers the mail to a mailroom in the building, and internal mail staff distributes the mail to employees' offices. The addresses of these employees are not routable by the post office, but they are very routable within the business enterprise.

When a home or office has more computers than public IP addresses, each computer typically is assigned a private IP address. For ease of management, low cost, and for security, we strongly recommend that your computers share a single public IP address, and that they not directly connect to the Internet. Private IP addresses hide the computers in home and office networks from the Internet.

---

[1] Actually, there is another set of private IP addresses, those starting with 10, for example, 10.0.1.3. Large corporations that hide the IP address of their computers use so-called "net 10" addresses. We do not use them here.

3-1-4 Packets and routing

The Internet equivalent of a letter or package is known as a **packet**. It is easiest to think of a packet as having a section called the **header** containing information about the IP addresses of the sender (source) and receiver (destination), and a section called the **body** containing the message content destined to the recipient. Think of the header as outside of the envelope of a letter, with the message body or content being the pages inside the envelope.

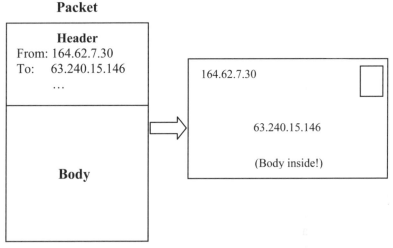

Packet

Figure 3-1: IP packet, also shown as an envelope

The magic of the Internet is based in part on the fact that delivery of packets (and hence the delivery of messages and content) depend only on destination and source information contained in the header of the packet. This should not seem strange, since the post office works the same way: they do not look inside the letter to determine how to deliver it. They only look at the outside of the envelope.

Like the post office, the Internet has formal limits on how big or small a packet can be. These limits ensure that some messages do not tie up unfair amounts of Internet resources. This means that long messages (say, big downloads) are broken up automatically into smaller packets by the network hardware and software of the sending computer, and are automatically reassembled by the network hardware and software of the receiving computer.

Let us follow a packet through the Internet. We use a simplified view of the Internet pictured in *Figure 3-2*.

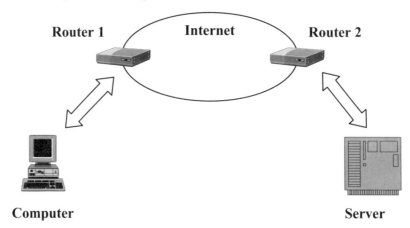

Figure 3-2: Simple network with computers and routers

In this figure, we show two kinds of devices: computers and **routers**. Routers are special purpose computers whose function is to correctly and efficiently route or pass Internet packets. You can think of them as the Internet equivalent of post offices and mailrooms.

When a router receives a packet, it uses the destination IP address in the packet's header to determine how to process or forward the packet. An address is **routable** if a router can determine how to process it. If the IP address is routable, the router will be able to make the correct choice on where to send the packet. For addresses that are not routable (e.g., if they are private), the router can make no decision, and it just discards the packet.

We demonstrate some of these ideas with an example: a computer "sending" a packet to a "receiving" computer as shown in *Figure 3-3*. To be specific, our source computer has IP address 164.62.7.30, and sends an IP packet to the destination computer whose IP address is 66.77.65.231.

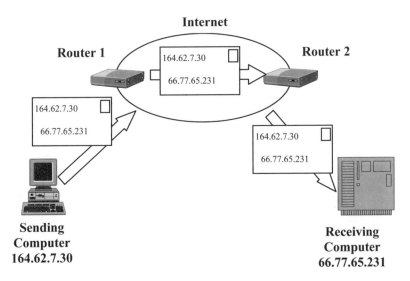

Figure 3-3: IP packet as it is routed through the network

As is typically the case, the sending computer will need "help" from the intermediate routers to deliver this packet. Here, router 1 receives the IP packet and determines that the packet's destination IP address is routable, and forwards the packet to router 2. This router now receives the IP packet and determines that it can route the packet. In fact, it knows exactly how to deliver this packet to the receiving computer at IP address 66.77.65.231.The receiving computer receives the IP packet and determines that it originated from the sending computer with address 164.62.7.30. It has taken three "hops" (or steps) to deliver this packet. In general, it can take tens of hops to deliver packets for a distantly connected destination.

That is all you need to know about packet delivery on the Internet.

3-1-5   IP names & Domain Name Service

The use of names greatly simplifies our daily lives. Imagine having to refer to "the restaurant at 357 Park Place" instead of "Joe's Diner," or not being able to refer to "the mall" or "Mom's house." One of the "almost magical" features of the Internet is its ability to allow the use of names for computers, services, and resources. Remember, we defined names as agreed upon descriptions for things.

When we want to access a computer on the Internet, we are free to use its IP address (for example, `66.77.65.231`), or we can use a name that has been created for it (in this case, `www.irs.gov`). Names are great conveniences: they are easier to remember, certainly more descriptive, and most importantly, they remain valid even if the IP address of the site has changed. There are many reasons why an IP address might change: the computer may have moved from one part of the country to another, the information it stores may have moved to a larger computer, or it may have failed and another computer is providing service in the meantime. The use of names instead of addresses provides this flexibility and capability.

IP names have structure to them; that is, they use a standard form and style. First, an IP name is a string of nonblank characters. Second, they have "parts," that is, words separated by periods, for example, `www.irs.gov`. This structure is important; each part is more specific then the one following it (reading from left to right). In this example, "`.gov`" describes all the computers in the government's network (actually, the U.S. government's network). "`irs.gov`" describes the computers in the Internal Revenue Service's network, certainly a subset of the entire government's network of computers. Finally, `www.irs.gov` describes the computer server that provides Web service (browsing) for the IRS.

There are limited (but growing) set of valid words that can be used as the final segment of an IP name. They are called **top level domains**. You are probably familiar with some of them. For example, `.com`, `.edu`, `.gov`, `.org`, and `.net` describe networks of companies, schools, government agencies, non-profit organizations, and network providers, respectively. There are some new ones, e.g., `.name`, `.info`, and `.biz`. You can find a list of the currently supported top-level domains in `www.iana.org/gtld/gtld.htm`. Finally, there are two letter combinations used to denote the networks of countries: for example, `.uk`, `.ru`, `.ca`, `.fr`, and `.jp` denote the networks of the United Kingdom, the Russian Federation, Canada, France, and Japan, respectively. You can find a list of all the currently supported country codes in `www.iana.org/cctld/cctld-whois.htm`. There is a two-letter code for the United States, `.us`, but it is infrequently used.

Within a particular "domain" (e.g., `irs.gov` or `intel.com`), the choice of more specific names is up to administrator of that domain. Therefore, there can be many computers named `www`, one in each domain (e.g., `www.irs.gov` and `www.intel.com`). This should be no surprise: there are many people called John or Richard. We use other information, such as middle and last names, to provide needed uniqueness.

OK, let us agree that IP names are the way to go. However, that leaves two big questions. First, since the routers that comprise the Internet direct packets based on IP addresses, not IP names, something must convert an IP name to its corresponding IP address. How is this done? Second, we described the benefits of being able to change the address associated with a name. With the millions of computers and names on the Internet, how is this done?

The answers to these questions are provided by a wonderful facility of the Internet known as **Domain Name Service** or **DNS**. DNS consists of software that runs as part of the systems software of your computers and a mesh of servers distributed throughout the Internet. Altogether, all these elements of DNS support the total collection of Internet names, translating each to its IP address.

There is not "one big DNS server." Instead, DNS divides the information among many computers spread out throughout the world. No matter what the name or no matter where the "lookup" request comes from, once any DNS server properly receives the request, DNS should provide the correct IP address.

When you attempt to reach an Internet computer by its IP name, the DNS software running on your computer attempts to translate the IP name into an IP address by sending a request (a packet) to a DNS server. (Don't worry, the IP address of this "DNS server" is part of the information provided to you or to your computer by your network service provider). As an example, suppose you wanted to browse the website `www.irs.gov`. Your computer would launch a query to the local DNS server asking for the IP address of `www.irs.gov`.

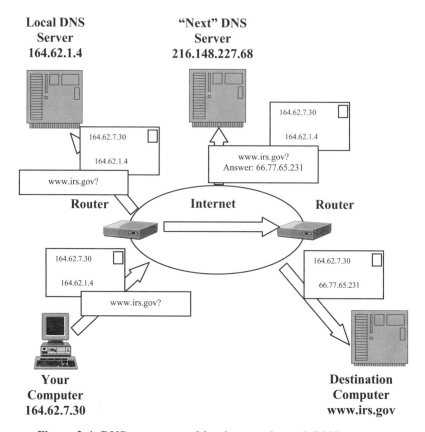

Figure 3-4: DNS request working its way through DNS system

The local DNS server receives this packet and works to obtain the answer. That means it will provide the answer if known, or it will provide as a partial answer the IP address of the "next" DNS server that should know the answer. With this information, your computer's DNS software can then reissue the request to that "next" DNS server. Eventually, either a server returns a valid address, or there is no matching IP address for it (for example, you may have typed in the wrong name). In this example, a DNS server finally returns the "answer," namely 66.77.65.231.

Your computer and the DNS servers send and receive all of these packets in the background. Sometimes, when there are delays in displaying the web page on your computer screen, your computer is waiting for DNS to return the IP address of the requested website.

Under the covers, your computer has done quite a bit of work on your behalf. It now knows the legitimate IP address for your packet. Your computer inserts this as the destination IP address for subsequent packets to this destination.

Most of the time, the servers you communicate with do not need to "look you up" to reply to your requests, since you provided your IP address as the return address in each packet. To reply to a request it just uses the source address in each response to you.

3-1-6   URLs

Universal Resource Locator or **URL** is the name of an item on an Internet server you can access from your web browser. These names provide a simple and uniform way to request all sorts of web content: web pages, downloadable files, pictures, and the like.

As an example, consider the URL

```
http://www.irs.gov/pub/irs-soi/02tc18fy.xls
```

This names a particular file or piece of content (pub/irs-soi/02tc18fy.xls) on a particular computer (`www.irs.gov`), and it provides the browser with instructions on how to retrieve it (use the Hypertext Transfer Protocol, or `http`). We would get the same result if we had replaced the IP name with an IP address. So

```
http://66.77.65.231/pub/irs-soi/02tc18fy.xls
```

would yield the same result.

3-2   LANs, workgroups, mini-internets and WANs

Each networked company, school, business, or home starts with computers connected together into local networks called **Local Area Networks** or **LANs**. The most common way to form LANs is to use Ethernet technology. Ethernet is the name of the data communication standard that applies mainly to LANs. It is relatively simple to create

LANs of reasonable size (say, from a few to a few hundred computers). In fact, your home or office network will be a LAN!

The resources connected by a LAN, such as computers, shared devices (such as printers and CD-readers), and applications need to be managed and protected to operate effectively together. This aggregation of resources has several commonly used names. Microsoft® uses two different names, **workgroup** and **domain**, and several other names are used in other contexts. In this book, we use the term **mini-internet** to describe the network, computers, devices, and applications that you need to configure, manage, and secure consistently.

Within a mini-internet, you can easily set things up to allow a user on one computer to use (or share) the printers and files on another. This means that the computers, printers, and peripherals that form a mini-internet become a group of computing resources that each user can share. In order to set this up, your mini-internet and each of its computers will need unique names. These names should be easier to remember than their IP addresses.

Most Windows-based computers start out with a default name of "My Computer" and some default workgroup name (e.g. WORKGROUP, HOME, or HOMENET). If you intend to share printers or files, you will need to assign each computer a unique name and the same workgroup name. This is not difficult. If you start with a brand new computer, part of the automatic network setup process will ask you to assign a computer name and workgroup name. If you have computers that are not "brand new," do not fret; we provide details on computer and workgroup naming in *Section 12-1*.

A magical thing about Internet technology is that the same technology used to form Local Area Networks can form networks of networks. **Wide Area Networks** or **WANs** are networks that cover a large geographic area (say, a university campus, a corporation, a city, a state, and a country). They are formed by connecting together numerous Local Area Networks to create a larger and larger network (see *Figure 3-5*).

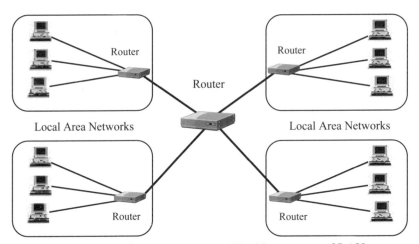

Figure 3-5: Wide Area Network (WAN) as group of LANs

The **Internet** is one such global WAN. Anytime you connect a computer to the Internet, it can access any other connected computer or server. This means that the Internet connects the largest community of computers and services. People want their computers to connect to it to access all the offered services. Providers of services want to connect to it to offer their services to the widest possible audience.

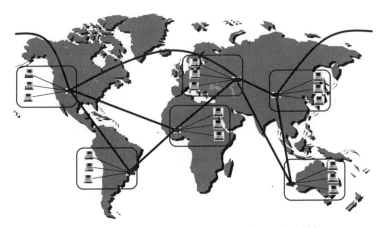

Figure 3-6: The Internet - the ultimate WAN

Specialized service providers, called **Internet Service Providers (ISPs)**, have evolved to provide customers like us access to the Internet. They allow you to connect to their service and send IP packets to them. They in turn agree to pass on these packets to the Internet and return responses from the Internet to you.

To connect to an ISP, you need to use a path that allows you to send IP packets. There are various ways to do this, including dialup phone connections, permanent connections such cable or DSL, even wireless (i.e. radio) connections.

Most of us have connected to the Internet using dialup connections, and most computers come with built-in dialup capability. Dialup connections can support a range of bandwidths, but cannot exceed about 5300 characters per second. That may seem like a lot, but it is not enough for browsing many websites. Typical web pages can have hundreds of thousands of characters in them, requiring many minutes to download. This means you wait a long time for your computer to display the page.

Newer services on the Internet allow you to download pictures and music. These files can be quite large; it is typical for a music file to be over 5 million characters (5MB) in length. It would take more than sixteen minutes at typical dialup rates to complete a download like this. Moreover, additional packet overheads and normal network congestion can slow things even more, so your wait could be half an hour or more.

Obviously, something faster would be much better. Permanent, broadband connections over cable or DSL are just that. These connections usually support speeds greater than 150,000 characters per second[2], or more than twenty five times faster than the fastest dialup connection. If you are lucky, cable or DSL may provide even faster service than this.

With such a high-speed connection, web page, file, and email downloads can take a fraction of the time it would take over dialup connections. (The 5 million-character music download would take just about 30 seconds). Also, and equally important, these connection are "always online." You do not need to "dialup" or disconnect. You are always online and therefore you do not need to waste time establishing a

---

[2] We arrive at this figure by dividing the claimed bandwidth (1.5 million bits per second) by 10. This takes into account overheads, and is usually a good estimate.

connection to the Internet. Because you are "always online," you need to pay special attention to the security of your mini-internet.

3-3   What is a voice, DSL, or cable modem?

When a computer communicates with another computer, its internal signals are not directly useful on phone lines or networks. It needs a device to translate its internal signals to an appropriate form for communication.

A **modem** is a device that converts computer messages to the form needed by the connection. Actually, modem is shorthand for "modulator-demodulator," but nobody uses this terminology anymore.

A **voice modem** (or **analog modem**) is used to connect computers using phone lines. They convert bits and bytes to sounds and tones, and transmit them over a phone connection. When they receive sounds and tones, they do the opposite: they convert sounds and tones to bits and bytes. You have probably heard the warble of a voice modem at work.

DSL modems and **cable modems** do similar work for DSL and cable connections, respectively. They do not actually convert the bits and bytes from the computer to tones and sounds, but they convert them to the appropriate electrical signals needed by the transmission medium: coax cables in the case of cable modems, and phone lines for DSL modems.

Which kind of modem do you need? It depends on the type of connection you are getting: if you are subscribing to DSL, you will need a DSL modem; if you are subscribing to cable service, you will need a cable modem. If you do not have one of these choices, then you will have to settle for a voice modem.

3-4   Wireless – How does it work?

Advances in radio and antenna technology, and the continued reduction in the cost of integrated circuits have made wireless networks a realistic alternative. Wireless allows quick and "cable-free" installations, accommodating those locations or circumstances where it is inconvenient to run cables. Wireless can work with both DSL and cable connections.

Wireless networks replace some wired components used in building a LAN with wireless components using radio technology. A "wireless" computer transmits and receives IP packets using a small radio device on a specialized wireless card. Wireless devices manage wireless connections by converting packets to the appropriate radio signals. In reverse, they receive radio signals, and convert them into packets.

During the last few years, the manufacturers of computer hardware, software, and wireless devices reached agreement on a broad range of wireless standards. The name of the most appropriate one for home and office networking is 802.11b. Wireless components that adhere to this standard from different manufacturers should work together. This means you can purchase components with confidence; they should work with any other wireless devices you may already have.

Wireless networks do present some issues. First, although the cost of wireless technology has been dropping, it is still more expensive than wired. Second, wired technology supports higher bandwidth and tends to be more predictable. Third, once in place, few environmental factors can disrupt wired communications. However, certain environmental factors can cause radio interference and can disrupt a wireless network that was previously functioning. Potential disruptors include physical objects (e.g., metal beams in walls and floors, air conditioners, water tanks and pipes) or other electronic devices (e.g., other wireless devices, microwave ovens, television sets, large speakers, etc.). Finally, wireless technology is evolving rapidly, and new faster standards are becoming available. Devices that adhere to these newer standards may not work with 802.11b devices.

We recommend the following rule: if you can easily wire or cable your devices, do so. If you cannot, or if mobility is an important feature within your mini-internet, then wireless presents a straightforward solution.

3-5   The Web – How does it work?

The **Web** is the collection of information and services that is generally accessible from the Internet. This collection includes

- information servers (e.g., servers that provide web pages to your browser)

- commerce servers (e.g., the servers that allow you to purchase or order things)
- interactive servers (e.g., servers that support chat and discussion groups)
- communications servers (e.g., servers that link you and your messages to pagers, telephones, etc.).

Over the last few years, the amount of content, services, and the number of people using the Web have grown dramatically. Many large corporations generate substantial revenues while realizing significant reduction in their operating costs by using the Web and the Internet.

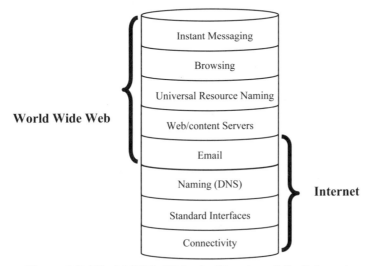

Figure 3-7: World Wide Web - built on top of the Internet

It would be difficult to imagine the World Wide Web without the Internet. There just is no other communications network with similar characteristics: ubiquity (that means its everywhere), scale (that means it grows to handle new traffic and new locations) and generality (that means that most applications "work" on it; it is not set up just to support a single application or service).

You can think of the Web as a "layer" on top of the Internet. It leverages the Internet's ability to send messages almost anywhere by building the kind of services that people want to use.

3-6   Email – How does it work?

Email, sending electronic "letters" or messages to named individuals, is just one kind of service supported by both the Internet and the World Wide Web.

Email services predated the evolution of the Web. They centered around two software programs, an **email server** and an **email client**. Email servers are programs that run on one or more computers that receive messages from users, store these messages to allow users to access them, and allow users to retrieve their messages. Email clients are programs that typically run on a user's personal computer, and that use the email server to send and receive email messages.

Prior to the Internet, each email client could connect only to a specific kind of email server. However, email standards are now very well established, and all of the popular clients and servers fully inter-work. Popular email clients are Microsoft Outlook™, Microsoft Outlook Express™, Netscape Messenger™, AOL Email[SM], and Eudora™. Popular email servers include Microsoft Exchange™ and Netscape Mail Server™. You do not need to worry about email servers. Your service provider has already selected one, and supports it for you. You can select the email client you prefer.

Email clients and email servers now all use the Internet to communicate. When your service is established, your provider will give you or let you choose your email "names." They will look something like johnsmith@bigprovider.com. The provider will set the "bigprovider.com" part: typically, it is the provider's name followed by ".com" or ".net." Your provider will also give you information you need to configure your email client. We cover that in more detail for one email client, Outlook Express, in *Section 17-15*.

3-7   Web based email

The Web created an opportunity to simplify how most people used email. It created "email without a client," that is, the ability to send and receive email messages using only your Web browser. You no longer need to install and configure an email client.

Web based email works by using your browser's ability to display pages and to submit forms to replace the special purpose email client. It looks just like surfing the Web. You surf to the URL of the website that provides your email to you, for example, "www.mail.com."

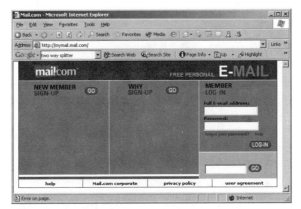

Figure 3-8: Access to web based email (courtesy of Mail.com™)

You "log in" to such services by providing your user name and password in the appropriate fields. The Web server then provides a page giving your customary email features and information.

3-8   Instant messaging

Instant messaging, as its name implies, is a way of sending messages to people almost instantaneously. If email is the electronic equivalent of sending letters or post cards, instant messaging is the equivalent of a telephone conversation.

To use instant messaging you must install an instant messaging client on your computer. Currently, the popular ones include AOL Instant Messenger^{SM} (AIM), Yahoo Messenger, and ICQ. Sometimes these programs come already installed when you purchase your computer.

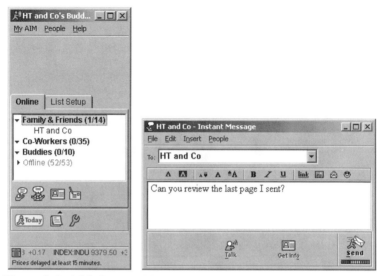

Figure 3-9: AOL Instant Messenger buddy list and message window

In order to communicate with a small group of friends, you maintain a "Buddy List:" a list of the name of people with whom you frequently keep in touch. The application indicates when these people are logged in and working on their computers, and therefore, when they may be available for conversations. Double-clicking on an active name brings up the message window, where you can type whatever short message you like. A message window with your message "pops up" on the recipient's computer screen. They can type responses in that window, and the instant messaging service quickly delivers that message to you.

To make this work, the application communicates over the Internet with an "instant messaging server." The server actually keeps track of the currently logged in users. Behind the scenes, frequent messages between the application running on your computer and the server assure that the "Buddy Window" indicates accurately who is active. When you send an instant message, your application actually sends it to the server, and the server forwards it to the desired recipient.

Instant messaging is an excellent way to keep in touch with friends, family, and co-workers!

3-9   *Bring your own access to AOL & MSN*

America On Line™ (AOL) and Microsoft Network™ (MSN) provide content and other features that are popular with consumers. Initially, both services provided dialup access; however, with the growing availability of broadband access, these services reduce charges for customers who use broadband instead of dialup access to reach them. As the name "Bring Your Own Access" (BYOA) implies, one can sign up for accessing these sites via a broadband connection instead of using a slow dialup connection.

In order for this to work, you need to sign up for the "Bring Your Own Access" service offered by these service providers. In addition, you need to change the settings of the associated client software to indicate that the access will use an Internet connection. In *Section 10-8*, we provide detailed instructions on how to change the settings of the AOL and MSN client application software.

What you should read next

If you are		Read next
	Someone wanting it "done for them"	Quickly browse *Chapter 4, Network Components*
	A novice	Quickly read *Chapter 4, Network Components*
	A typical user	Browse or skip *Chapter 4, Network Components*
	A power user	Quickly scan *Chapter 5, Planning for Broadband Service*

4

Network Components

You will be using simple, low cost, and readily available, off-the-shelf network components to create your home or office network. You will find these products easy to connect together. More importantly, once you have connected them into your home or office network, you will find that they require little or no attention. You may, most of the time, forget that they are even there.

In this chapter, we describe the network components you will likely need. In the following chapters, we present a straightforward set of steps to design, install, and configure your network. This includes help on selecting the types and number of components you will need.

Your network will need at least the following components: a cable or DSL modem to connect you to the Internet, a wired or wireless router to connect and secure your computers, a network adapter for each computer to enable communication, and RJ-45 cables to connect the wired components to each other.

4-1   Modems

Computers use **modems** to connect to the Internet. Modems take care of sending the bits and bytes of computer messages over telephone, DSL, or cable networks to a destination site that reverses this function and retrieves the original bits and bytes.

Figure 4-1: Typical external and internal voice modems

Figure 4-2: Typical PC card (PCMCIA) modem (courtesy of DLink®)

Voice modems connect computers through the telephone network. If you listen to these modems doing their work on your computer speakers, you will hear lots of beeps and chirps. Modems use tones and voices to do their work. The speeds that voice modems support are typically less that 53 Kilobits per second (about 5300 characters per second), and PCs and laptops usually have one. Most desktop PCs use modem cards that plug into internal PCI (Peripheral Component Interconnect) slots, standardized connectors for adding new components to the computer. Most desktop computers have 3 to 5 PCI slots. Some laptop computers use modems that install in a PC Card (PCMCIA) slot. The PC Card (PCMCIA) slots of laptops are standardized connectors that are readily accessible without the need for tools.

Figure 4-3: Typical cable modem

Cable modems use cable television wires to support high-speed connections to the Internet (typically, 1.5 Megabits per second or about 150,000 characters per second). Although some new PCs have cable modems already installed, a separate standalone cable modem is a better choice for flexibility in home and office networking. A cable modem that is built into a PC requires that PC to be powered in order for other computers to use the broadband connection.

Figure 4-4: Typical DSL modem

DSL modems use existing telephone wires for high-speed connections (typically, between 20,000 and 150,000 characters per second) to the Internet. New PCs sometimes have built-in DSL modems. However, a separate standalone DSL modem is a better choice for flexibility in home and office networking. A DSL modem that is built into a PC requires that PC to be powered in order for other computers to use the broadband connection.

Newer cable and DSL modems are equipped with Ethernet (RJ-45) and USB jacks. Since you will not connect your computer directly to the cable or DSL modem, beware of earlier modems that only supported USB connections. We do not use them in the configurations described in this book.

The price of cable or DSL modems ranges from of $50 to $150, but in most instances, the cable or DSL service provider lease these devices to you for a small monthly fee.

4-2   Routers

The Internet uses routers extensively to move packets of information around the country and around the globe. They connect the various Internet devices (e.g., computers, other routers, and other network components) together by "routing" (or passing) IP packets. Routers do this task very efficiently and reliably.

Figure 4-5: Typical home/office router

Home and office networks can take advantage of router technology to build a network, providing the sophistication and convenience previously only found in corporate intranets: large companies' internal data networks.

The size of current home/office routers is comparable to a hand held CD player or small book. These routers act as the focal point connecting the home or office network to the wider global Internet. They enforce security on your network by hiding the IP addresses of your computers, and filter some harmful traffic.

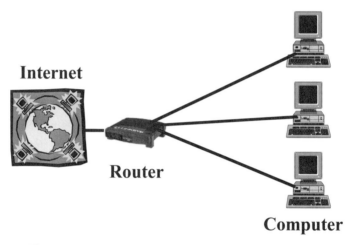

Figure 4-6: A router as the central point for computers

Home/office routers currently cost between $60 and $150. The cost varies based on whether it supports wireless connections and on the number of jacks (or **ports**). In a later paragraph, we describe the kinds of wires and connectors used to connect to routers. At this point, it suffices to say that home/office routers concentrate all network connections in the home or office.

4-3   Hubs and switches

What do you do if you have more computers that there are ports in your router? You need the network equivalent to the electric "power strip," that is, something that can plug into a single router port and present many more ports. A hub or switch is the requisite device.

Figure 4-7: A five-port switch

The **hub** is a device that connects computers to each other or to a router. A hub simply replicates the packets it receives from one computer, and makes them available to the other computers. Hubs are rated in terms of the speeds (typically, 10 or 100 Megabits per second) and by the number of ports they support.

A **switch** is a more intelligent device than a hub since it allows simultaneous interactions between multiple computers. On a busy mini-internet, a switch can double or triple the network performance over a hub.

In home and small office applications, hubs or switches that support 4 to 8 ports and cost between $20 and $50 are usually adequate. The size of a hub or switch is the size of a hand held CD player or book. For larger networks, one may want to use 12- to 24-port switches or hubs.

Whereas hubs support one "interaction between computers" at a time, switches can support several. If your mini-internet needs the use of a switch or hub, all things being equal, choose the switch. If you find that hubs are significantly less expensive, choose hubs.

For simplicity in the remainder of the book, we use the term "switch" to mean either a switch or hub.

4-4   Ethernet network adapters

In order to connect to the routers and switches, computers use Ethernet cards, referred to as **network adapters** in computer jargon. Network adapters support high-speed connections of 10, 100, or 1000 Megabits per second, all are more than adequate speeds to support the movements of files within the home or office. You will find an internal network adapter already installed in most computers.

Figure 4-8: Typical network adapters – wired, wireless, and USB

In most cases, you do not need to install a network adapter. Your computer already has one. If you cannot determine whether your computer has one, please check *Section 17-8-1*.

If you have an older PC or laptop that has no network adapter, you will need to install one. Which kind depends on the type of computer you have, and your ability to install an internal network adapter. Before buying a network adapter, it is important to check the computer manual to see what internal slots it supports. The slots are standardized connectors for adding new components to the computer. Most desktop computers have 3 to 5 PCI slots. Laptop computers have slots called PCMCIA slots that allow easy insertion of the credit card sized network adapters (called PC Card) into the laptop. Here is a flowchart providing guidance.

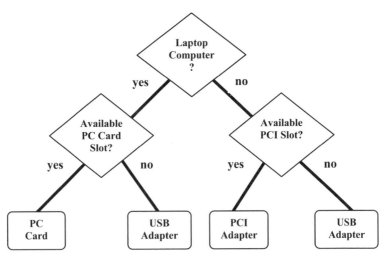

Figure 4-9: Selecting a network adapter

If you have a desktop PC with no network adapter and you can install a PCI network adapter, then it is your best choice. A PCI network adapter is the cheapest ($10-$20) and best performing. If you have a laptop with no network adapter, and you can install a PC Card (PCMCIA) network adapter, then this is your best choice ($40-$80). Otherwise, or if you do not want to open the computer case to install an internal adapter, you could use a USB network adapter. It is easy to install and is midway in cost between a PCI and PC Card (PCMCIA). If your computer is very old, or is running Windows 98 First Edition, it may not have a functioning USB port and therefore you need to find out what other kind of slots it has and install that kind of network adapter.

4-5   How do I connect these things?

Key concerns in building your network are the placement of your computers and network components (e.g., router), and how you "connect" them together. You have a choice of two methods to connect: wired and wireless.

Wireless installations generally are easier, since there are no cables to lay and secure. They can be a bit more expensive, and it is possible that they will not work well in some homes or office buildings.

Wired installations can be less expensive and robust, but cabling can be a big issue. It may not be easy to run cables safely and securely.

4-5-1   Wireless networking

Wireless networking is a convenience that avoids the physical wiring connecting computers, switches, and routers. Wireless routers and wireless network adapters replace the wired version described above. Invariably, these devices are a bit more expensive than the wired types, and they do not work properly or reliably in some home or office setups.

Wireless communication is sensitive to environmental factors, such as microwave ovens, that sometimes lead to erratic performance or no performance at all. In most instances, you do not move desktop computers around the home or office, so having a physical connection is the best and cheapest choice.

Figure 4-10: Typical wireless devices

There are circumstances where cabling is just not practical. For example, you may have no safe or attractive route for cabling. In addition, a special area of use for wireless networks may be to extend wired networks for laptops. If you can accept the additional cost, or if your circumstances demand it, we recommend the use of wireless network components. In most cases, 802.11b wireless components install easily and work well.

One area of concern with wireless networks is the ability of hackers to eavesdrop or access the Internet through your network. To prevent this, you must make sure that the connections between the router and the wireless network adapters are secure. We show you how to set up the network correctly.

4-5-2   RJ-45 for Ethernet/computer networking

Standard Ethernet cables connect the modem, router and wired switches and computers. The current generation of Ethernet cables is called CAT-5E for enhanced category 5 cables. They can typically support connections of 10, 100, or 1000 Megabits per second (10Mb/s, 100 Mb/s, or 1000Mb/s).

Figure 4-11: RJ-45 jack and connector

Most Ethernet cables, including the older CAT-5 or CAT-3 cables, are adequate for home or office use. The simplest approach is to purchase cables with RJ-45 connectors of appropriate lengths, and use them to connect the router, switches, and computers. In this arrangement, there is no need to cut an Ethernet cable or add connectors to it. The switches and routers come with standard jacks that accept RJ-45 connectors.

 You will sometimes see an Ethernet cable with RJ-45 connectors labeled as a **crossover Ethernet cable** This is a special cable whose wires are connected to the RJ-45 connectors in such a way as to flip the transmit and receive signals between the devices. Our layouts and designs use only standard or **straight through** cables. A simple way to tell if a particular cable is a crossover cable is to hold both connectors next to each other with the metal contacts pointing of each "pointing up." Looking carefully, you should be able to see the colors of the small wires that makeup the cable. If the sequence of colored wires are the same in both connectors (i.e. orange-white, orange, blue-white, blue, etc.) then you have a straight through cable. If the color sequence is different, you have a crossover cable. If you follow our guidance, you will not need a crossover Ethernet cable. However, if you are upgrading an existing network, you may encounter crossover Ethernet cables.

We strongly recommend using the newer CAT-5E cabling in new construction or in the walls of the house or office. If you are doing this, you can install, or have a licensed electrician install, a set of RJ-45 jacks at all the proper places.

The most important idea here is that every computer in the network must have a network adapter, and if wired, an RJ-45 Ethernet cable connecting it to the rest of the network. Therefore, a printer or any other device without an RJ-45 jack does not connect to your network. It connects to a computer that must connect to the network.

4-5-3   RJ-11 for phones and faxes

Most homes and offices already come wired for phone service, so why not use these wires for connecting network components and computers? Part of the reason is that phone wires are not designed to carry high-speed data traffic. Buildings frequently use several types of phone wire and have many phone outlets. These can cause problems when used for high-speed data traffic.

Numerous industry groups are working on high speed data product specifications for home and office phone wiring. In the near future, technical advances may allow easier and more cost effective use of a building's phone wiring. Until then, we believe that RJ-45 Ethernet cables or 802.11b wireless components currently provide a cheaper, easier to use and more robust solution in most circumstances.

Figure 4-12: RJ-11 jack and connector

DSL modems split the phone connection coming into the home or office into a "plain old telephone" connection (an RJ-11 jack) and a data connection (an RJ-45 jack). The home or office telephones connect to the RJ-11 "plain old telephone" jacks. The data network connects to the RJ-45 jack using an RJ-45 Ethernet cable. DSL technology allows the simultaneous use of the telephone, fax, and data transmission because the modem uses different frequency ranges for each.

4-6   Power conservation techniques

You will find that the best way of powering a number of computers, printers and other devices together is to use power strips, available at a local home supply or electronic retailer. In most instances, you will need power strips that allow 5 to 6 electric outlets for powering the computer, printers, loudspeakers, and other peripherals. We strongly recommend that you buy power strips with surge protection to protect your computers and peripherals from spikes and surges. Power strips usually come with a switch that allows you to turn the power on and off to all devices connected to it. This feature may come in handy in conserving electricity when the computer and its peripherals are not in use.

Some more expensive power strips are equipped with a battery that gives limited backup in case your power fails. The battery backup feature only protects against brief power outages and is most useful in powering your modem, router, and computers.

Computers, printers, routers, and other electronic devices use an appreciable amount of electricity when left powered all the time. A typical PC consumes about the same amount of electricity as a 100-watt light bulb. With printers, monitor and other peripherals, the total can probably double. Powered continuously, a typical PC with its peripherals could consume about 2-4 kilowatt-hours per day. At a national average rate of about 10 cents per kilowatt-hour, running a computer constantly can cost you between $6 and $12 per month.

In order to conserve electricity we recommend that you power your computers only when you are using them, but that you power the network components, that is, the router, DSL, or cable modem, and switches continuously. This ensures your network is readily available to access the Internet whenever you need it. In addition, we recommend that you connect each computer and all of its peripherals on its own separate power strip. This will allow you to turn the computer and all its peripherals off easily when not needed.

 Remember to wait for the computer to shut down before you turn the power off. This will avoid problems with your computer.

What you should read next

If you are	Read next
Someone wanting it "done for them"	*Chapter 5, Planning for Broadband Service*
A novice	*Chapter 5, Planning for Broadband Service*
A typical user	Quickly browse *Chapter 5, Planning for Broadband Service*
A power user	Quickly scan *Chapter 5, Planning for Broadband Service*

Part 2
Building Your Network

5

Planning for Broadband Service

It is possible that you already have cable or DSL broadband service in your home or office. If that is the case, you can safely skip to the next chapter, where we go through the steps of designing your network.

This chapter discusses some of the issues you need to consider prior to obtaining service and helps you select a broadband service provider.

5-1 Locating broadband service providers in your area

If you are lucky, there will be at least two broadband service providers serving your home or office. Most likely, one will base their service on cable TV technology, the other on DSL technology.

The cable TV provider in your area is likely the company that provides broadband cable modem service. The largest cable providers are AT&T Comcast (www.attbroadband.com or www.comcast.com), AOL Time Warner/RoadRunner (www.rr.com), and Cox (www.cox.com). If you can connect to the Internet, you should visit their websites to see if they provide cable modem service in your area (you need to provide your zip code). If you have no current Internet service, we recommend you visit your library to complete these searches.

The largest DSL provider in your area is likely your local telephone company. Contact them to see if DSL service is available to your location. This depends on your specific address and other factors. You can find links or phone number of smaller DSL providers or resellers in the phone book or at computer and electronic retailers.

You can also visit our website, www.BooksInAFlash.com, for help in locating a provider in your area.

5-2   Selecting a broadband service provider

The choice between cable and DSL service is not always an easy one. There are three important factors, however, that may help you decide: performance, cost, and reliability.

Broadband cable service usually provides consistent and speedy performance to all customers (typically 1.5 Mb/sec "downstream" and 150Kb/s "upstream"). This performance may degrade if there are many users in your neighborhood during peak periods. The performance of DSL service can vary widely, based on distance from the service office. Other factors being roughly equal, you should select the provider that can provide the fastest service to you. Asking your neighbors about their experience with a service is a good indication of the performance you will experience.

If you have a choice of broadband service providers, it is likely that competition will work to level the prices. You will likely not see much difference for "basic" service offerings. However, it is possible that there will be substantial differences in the cost of installation, the cost of modems, etc. Choose accordingly.

It is unlikely that the reliability of basic broadband access service will vary between the providers. In earlier days, both sets of providers had growing pains. However, there should not be much difference here, especially if there is competition in your area.

Therefore, it is likely that you have to choose mostly based on the price of the service and of the installation. The answer, therefore, is easy: get service from the cheapest provider of the fastest service.

6

Planning Your Network

Once you have decided which broadband service provider to use, you should contact them to get pricing, availability, and installation options. Armed with this information, you can make informed choices about what to obtain from the provider and what you need to purchase.

With this information in hand, you can create the plan for your home or office network. You do this in two main steps. First, you create a "layout" of your computers and related items showing their rough location within the building. Second, you create a network "design" showing the specific network components you will be using (e.g., router, switches, and cables). In fact, you will be determining the extent to which you will be using wired or wireless elements.

If you know that you want a wireless network, you can quickly skip some of the work described in this chapter. Otherwise, we show you how to assess the details of your network to determine quickly your network design.

You need to have an overall plan on how to connect everything within your mini-internet. We call this overall plan your network layout. The layout will show all network components connected with lines of various colors, each representing a wireless link or RJ-45 Ethernet cable. For wired links, this is the time to determine the ease and practicality of running these cables, and if possible, to determine the cable's actual path.

It is possible that there is no easy way of running one or more of the cables. For example, your computers may be on different floors of your home, or there may not be an easy way to run the cables safely. In such a case, either you must hire a professional to run the wires in your walls, or you need to use wireless "connections."

If you can find a potential path for the cables, it is important to examine each cable's actual path. This is important for several reasons. First, the cable's actual route will most likely not be the most direct route between the two network components. Most often, something will be in the way: a wall, a heavily trafficked hallway, furniture, or even one or more floors or ceilings. Second, the appropriate length of each cable will depend on its actual path, including the distance from desk to floor and back. (In fact, it is normally a safe practice to add about six to ten feet to the measured distance to allow for the actual placement of the cable.) If you ignore these factors, you almost certainly will purchase cables that will be too short.

In some circumstances, a "round about" route is the most practical one. Why worry about cables that someone might walk on, trip over, or inadvertently pull. Each run of a CAT-5E cable can be up to one hundred meters (about 328 feet), so you can take a safe or easy "round about" route.

Although it is difficult to give a hard and fast rule to determine the type of network to design, we recommend the following process:

- Explore all reasonable options to run your cables safely. This usually yields the lowest cost, most robust and secure installation.
- If you cannot reasonably place one or more cables, cost out your network using wireless components for those computers and compare it to the cost of network installation by a professional.
- If your computers are very widely spread apart, or if you have a requirement for supporting "mobility," you need a wireless network.
- If you have a very simple layout, for example, several computers relatively close together, and you are willing to trade some increase in cost for ease of installation, go for wireless.

We describe standard layouts and designs: two wired and one wireless configuration. We believe your design will closely match one of these. If yours is an unusual case, you certainly will be able to extend one of our designs to fit your situation.

Here are the steps you will complete in this chapter:

1. Create an inventory of your computers, printers and other devices.

2. Create an initial layout by placing these resources where you want them.

3. Match your network characteristics to one of the three network configurations that we give in this chapter. Using the proper template, finish the layout process and complete the design stage.

4. Create a list of all network components and cables needed for your network.

6-1   Creating an inventory

First, start by listing the computers that you currently have in your home or office. Then list all the printers and other devices that connect to these computers. *Table 6-1* is an example of how to do this.

Description of Computer	Name of Computer	Description of Printer	Location
HP Pavilion 700	Harry-HP1	HP Color DeskJet	First floor office
HP Pavilion 300	John-HP2		John's room
Dell Dimension 4300	Mary-Dell1	HP LaserJet 5L	Mary's room
Gateway Solo 1400LS	Pat-GW1		Den

Table 6-1: Inventory of computers, printers and other devices

Here we have picked computer names that indicate the computer manufacturer as well as the first name of the main user. This approach may make sense in a home. In an office setting, you may want to use a different approach to identify each computer connected to your network.

Appendix A-3 contains a template you may copy to help you make this list. In addition, you will find Microsoft Word and HTML formatted templates on www.BooksInAFlash.com.

6-2   Creating a layout of your network

We assume that you have an idea where you would like the cable or DSL modem installed in your home or office. We show an example of a paper drawing that identifies the location of the cable or DSL modem, computers, printers, and scanners, based on the inventory created in the previous section. Prepare a similar drawing for items on your inventory. This drawing becomes the layout and inventory of computers printers and other devices in your network, as shown in *Figure 6-1*. You use this layout to create your network design.

All of our network configurations use a router to provide security and connectivity for your computers. Place a box near the modem to represent the router. Label it "router."

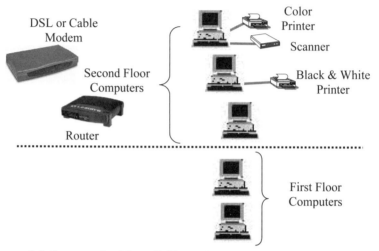

DSL or Cable Modem

Color Printer

Scanner

Second Floor Computers

Black & White Printer

Router

First Floor Computers

Figure 6-1: Layout of cable or DSL modem, computers, and other devices

6-3   Matching your network to the configurations

We describe three standard designs: two wired and one wireless. Your design should match closely one of these. Once you have selected one of the given templates, use the corresponding section to create a design and list of all components you need for your network. Even if yours is an unusual layout, you certainly should be able to extend one of the given layouts to fit. Otherwise, you need to ask for professional help.

For simplicity and ease of troubleshooting, we recommend the use of different colored RJ-45 Ethernet cables as described in *Table 6-2*. We represent the different cables as dots, solid or dashes lines in the figures.

Cable Color	Cable represented in figures	Cable end-points
GRAY	··················	Modem to router/switch
BLUE	——————————————	Router/switch to computers
RED	— — — — —	Router to switch

Table 6-2: Recommended cable colors

Using *Table 6-3*, match your network characteristics with the listed configurations and select the next section to read.

Network characteristics	Configuration	Described in Section
Up to 4 computers, can easily cable	Wired router, no switches	*Section 6-4*
Several to many computers "close together", can't cable	Wireless router	*Section 6-5*
Several to many computers on more than one floor or "far apart", can easily cable	Wired router, switches	*Section 6-6*

Table 6-3: Configuration instructions

6-4   *Network for several wired computers*

This section provides instructions for creating the layout and design of networks where cabling is not a problem, and where you have four or fewer computers, typically on the same floor as the cable or DSL modem. If this does not describe your situation, please refer to *Table 6-3* to locate the proper section to read.

In this simple arrangement, you need a wired router with at least four ports. Using the layout you created in *Section 6-2*, draw a solid line from each computer to the router to represent a blue cable. Connect the router to the modem using a dotted line to represent a gray cable. The figure below illustrates such an arrangement.

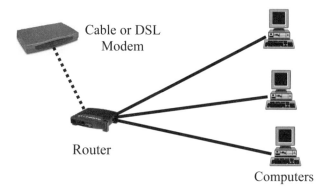

Figure 6-2: Simple layout of computers, router, and modem

To the best of your ability, estimate the length of each cable. Remember to increase your estimate for each cable by an additional six to ten feet to account for any indirect routes.

6-4-1 Creating your list

Now that you have a design, you are ready to create a list of components you need to purchase from a computer or electronic store.

Use the template in *Appendix A-4* to help you identify all the components and cables you need for your design. We show an example component list in *Table 6-4*. Remember to include in your list any network adapters and power strips you may need (refer to *Figure 4-9* for help).

ITEM	QUANTITY	LENGTH	DESCRIPTION
ROUTER	1		4- OR 8-PORT ROUTER
ETHERNET CABLE – GRAY CAT-5E	1	5 FT.	CONNECTS ROUTER TO CABLE OR DSL MODEM
ETHERNET CABLE – BLUE CAT-5E	1	50 FT.	CONNECTS COMPUTER TO ROUTER
ETHERNET CABLE – BLUE CAT-5E	1	25 FT.	CONNECTS COMPUTER TO ROUTER
ETHERNET CABLE – BLUE CAT-5E	1	5 FT.	CONNECTS COMPUTER TO ROUTER

Table 6-4: List of components for connecting 3 computers

That is it! Consult the table at the end of this chapter to continue.

6-5   *Network for wireless and wired computers*

This section provides instructions for creating the layout and design of networks where you have several to many computers, all within about 150 feet of each other, where some have no easy or practical cabling option. This means you will be using both wireless and wired components to create your network. If this does not describe your situation, please refer to *Table 6-3* to locate the proper section to read.

If your network is completely wireless, we recommend that you plan to connect a computer to the router using a RJ-45 Ethernet cable to simplify setting up your network. You can remove the cable and move the computer later. If this is not feasible, a completely wireless setup is possible, but you need to be extremely careful!

In this wireless arrangement, you need one wireless router and a wireless network adapter for each wireless computer. Using the layout you created in *Section 6-2*, place a figure to represent each wireless network adapter. For each wired computer, connect it to the router using a solid line to represent a blue cable. Draw a dotted line from the router to the cable or DSL modem to represent a gray cable. *Figure 6-3* illustrates such an arrangement.

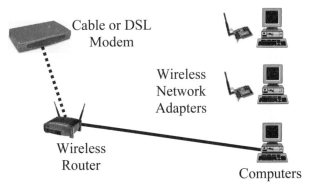

Figure 6-3: Simple layout of computers, wireless router, and modem

To the best of your ability, estimate the length of each cable. Remember to increase your estimate for each cable by an additional six to ten feet to account for any indirect routes.

6-5-1   Creating your list

Now that you have a layout, you are ready to create a list of components you need to purchase. If all your computers are wireless, we recommend that you buy one blue RJ-45 Ethernet cable to connect a computer to the cable or DSL modem during initial installation.

Use the template in *Appendix A-4* to help you identify all the components and cables you need for your design. We show an example component list in *Table 6-5*. Remember to include in your list any network adapters and power strips you may need (refer to *Figure 4-9* for help).

ITEM	QUANTITY	LENGTH	DESCRIPTION
WIRELESS ROUTER	1		4- OR 8-PORT WIRELESS ROUTER
ETHERNET CABLE – GRAY CAT-5E	1	5 FT.	CONNECTS ROUTER TO CABLE OR DSL MODEM
WIRELESS NETWORK ADAPTERS	2		CONNECTS COMPUTER TO ROUTER
ETHERNET CABLE – BLUE CAT-5E	1	15 FT.	CONNECTS COMPUTER TO ROUTER

Table 6-5: List of components for simple wireless layout

That is it! Consult the table at the end of this chapter to continue.

6-6   *Complex wired network*

This section provides instructions for creating the layout and design of networks where cabling is not a problem, and where you have many computers, typically on different floors or in different "regions" of the building. If this does not describe your situation, please refer to *Table 6-3* to locate the proper section to read.

If you have computers on multiple floors (or in different regions of a building) as shown in *Figure 6-4*, then we recommend that you connect computers on each floor or region to a switch. Using the layout you created in *Section 6-2*, insert the appropriate number of boxes in your drawing to represent the switches, and connect each computer to one with a solid line representing a blue cable. Then connect each switch to the router with a dashed line representing a red cable. Finally, connect the router to the cable or DSL Modem with a dotted line representing a gray cable. The *Figure 6-4* illustrates such an arrangement.

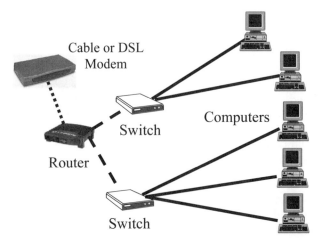

Figure 6-4: Layout of computers, router, switches, and modem

 To the best of your ability, estimate the length of each cable. Remember to increase your estimate for each cable by an additional six to ten feet to account for any indirect routes.

6-6-1   Creating your list

Now that you have a layout, you are ready to create a list of components you need to purchase.

Use the template in *Appendix A-4* to help you identify all the components and cables you need for your design. We show an example component list in *Table 6-6*. Remember to include in your list any network adapters and power strips you may need (refer to *Figure 4-9* for help).

That is it! Consult the table at the end of this chapter to continue.

ITEM	QUANTITY	LENGTH	DESCRIPTION
FLOOR ONE			
ROUTER	1		4- OR 8- PORT ROUTER
ETHERNET CABLE – GRAY CAT-5E	1	5 FT.	CONNECTS ROUTER TO CABLE OR DSL MODEM
SWITCH	1		4-8-PORT SWITCH
ETHERNET CABLE – RED CAT-5E	1	5 FT.	CONNECTS SWITCH TO ROUTER
ETHERNET CABLE – BLUE CAT-5E	1	25 FT.	CONNECTS COMPUTER TO SWITCH
ETHERNET CABLE – BLUE CAT-5E	1	25 FT.	CONNECTS COMPUTER TO SWITCH
ETHERNET CABLE – BLUE CAT-5E	1	5 FT.	CONNECTS COMPUTER TO SWITCH
FLOOR TWO			
SWITCH			4-8-PORT SWITCH
ETHERNET CABLE – RED CAT-5E	1	25 FT.	CONNECTS SWITCH TO ROUTER
ETHERNET CABLE – BLUE CAT-5E	1	25 FT.	CONNECTS COMPUTER TO SWITCH
ETHERNET CABLE – BLUE CAT-5E	1	5 FT.	CONNECTS COMPUTER TO SWITCH

Table 6-6: List of components for a complex configuration

What you should read next

If you are	Read next
Someone wanting it "done for them"	Browse *Chapter 7 (cable) or Chapter 8 (DSL)*
A novice	*Chapter 7 (cable) or Chapter 8 (DSL)*
A typical user	*Chapter 7 (cable) or Chapter 8 (DSL)*
A power user	Read quickly *Chapter 7 (cable) or Chapter 8 (DSL)*

7

Setting Up Cable Modem Service

This chapter provides the steps needed to get broadband service activated, if you are using a cable modem. If you are activating DSL service, you should skip to *Chapter 8, Setting Up DSL Modem Service*.

7-1   Contacting a cable provider

You need to sign up for broadband Internet service from your local cable provider. When you do this, you will find out details of the service, for example, when they will activate service, and whether the provider will install the cable modem for you. **If this is an option, we strongly recommend that you let the cable operator do this for you**. The installer will point out the entry location for the cable service, and ask you to indicate where you want the cable modem situated.

It is best to locate the cable modem near where you plan to locate your router and one of your computers, preferably one that is centrally located. We refer to this computer as the "first" computer. If you need to troubleshoot your network, having easy access to the router, cable modem, and "first" computer is a plus.

Initially, the installer or you set up the cable modem and the "first" computer to verify the broadband service. Later, you add the router and other computers to form your network.

The cable modem connects to the cable provider's network, just as your telephone connects to the telephone network. The place to make this connection to the broadband network is right at the point where the cable enters your home or office. If that is distant from where your cable modem needs to be, the installer will need to install coax cabling from the service entry to the cable modem.

In most instances, cable operators provide or rent the cable modem to you. They also provide without cost the additional hardware needed to make the cable modem connection operate properly. They may even connect it to one computer designated by you and install a network adapter if needed. In some instances, you may have to purchase the modem.

7-1-1   Installer sets up the modem

Here are the steps that you and the installer go through to set up the cable modem and your "first" computer, usually the computer closest to the cable modem.

 You collect the information in the templates in *Appendix A-2* and *Appendix A-5* from the installer. You will need this later to configure your computers and your router.

1. The installer verifies that your computer already has a network adapter, or installs one in your computer.

    The cable modem must support an RJ-45 Ethernet cable to your computer if you are to use it in your network. Most new cable modems support RJ-45 and USB connections, but some models only support a USB connection. **Do not accept a modem that only has a USB connection.**

2. The installer connects the installed network adapter to the cable modem using a blue RJ-45 Ethernet cable and power the cable modem.

3. When a computer's operating system detects the network adapter, it will automatically install a software driver for the network adapter. This software allows this computer to operate the network hardware properly. If the computer does not have the needed driver, the installer inserts a CD that contains it.

4. The installer very likely reboots your computer now. Next, the installer configures the Internet software (called TCP/IP).

    Most recent versions of Windows (e.g., Windows XP) include a **New Connection Wizard** that guides the installer through the steps of setting up the network adapter and TCP/IP. For older versions of

Windows (e.g., Windows 98), the installer may use a CD to install the necessary software.

5. If your service provider supports dynamic IP address assignment, your computer's networking parameters need to be set to use the **DHCP** protocol. If your provider uses static IP address assignment, make sure you record this information.

6. Ask the installer to set up your email account. This entails setting parameters for the email client that you plan on using. See *Sections 3-6* and *10-7*.

Installation should be complete. You should test the computer and the cable modem connection before the installer leaves. Make sure your browser can access the Internet, and that your email service is working. Just send an email message to yourself and see if you receive it. If all works well, you are ready to skip to *Chapter 9* where we walk you through the installation of your home or office network.

7-1-2   You set up the modem

Obtain from the cable operator or a local electronic store an approved cable modem, a two-way splitter (see *Figure 7-1*) and a length of coax cable suitable to connect the cable modem to the service entry.

The cable modem must have an RJ-45 Ethernet jack for your computer. Most new cable modems support RJ-45 and USB connections, but some models only support a USB connection. **Do not accept a modem that only has a USB connection**.

Figure 7-1: A two-way splitter

As the name implies, a two-way splitter is a simple device that splits one coax cable into two, which in this case, allows the cable to connect both to your television sets and to your new cable modem. Most of the time, cable operators give you the splitter and coax cable at no charge.

The best place of inserting the splitter is right at the point where the cable connection enters the home or office. Install the two-way cable splitter here. If you need to cut the cable in order to install the cable splitter, we recommend that you ask the cable operator to cut it and install the cable modem. If you have cut coax cable and successfully installed coax connectors before, then go ahead, cut the cable, install two coax connectors to the cut cable, and continue with the rest of this section.

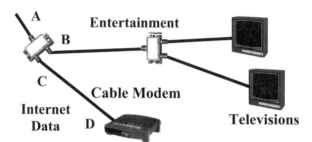

Figure 7-2: Cable modem and television sets connected to coax cable

Connect the incoming coax cable to the input jack of the splitter (A). Connect the existing video/TV cable to one of the splitter's output jacks (B). Connect the coax cable for the cable modem to the splitter's other output jack (C). Lay this run of coax from the splitter to the location of your cable modem and connect it to the cable modem (D). Congratulations! You have now completed this phase of the installation!

Turn each of your televisions on now, and check the picture. If the video reception on any of your television sets is noticeably worse, then check all the connections and make sure they are all tight. If the problem persists then we recommend that you call the cable company and ask them to check the strength of the signal entering the premises. Sometimes, you need to install an amplifier to improve the signal strength. Contact your cable company for information on type of amplifier and location.

Call the cable provider to activate your service. Give them the serial number and information to identify uniquely your cable modem on their network. In return, they tell you when the service will start. There is other information that you need to get from the cable company. Collect the information in the templates in *Appendix A-2* and *Appendix A-5*. You will need this later to configure your computers and your router.

You must ask the service provider whether they support static or dynamic IP address assignment. If static, you must obtain from the provider the following information: your static IP address, your subnet mask, the IP address of the default gateway, and the IP address (or addresses) of the DNS.

Here are the steps that you must go through to set up the cable modem and your "first" computer, usually the computer closest to the cable modem.

Verify that your computer already has a network adapter. Most recently manufactured computers come with one. If your computer does not have a network adapter, you must install one. Refer to the flowchart in *Figure 4-9* to guide your selection.

1. First, shut your computer down normally. If your computer has a network adapter, skip to the next step. Otherwise, unplug the computer's power cord.

   To install a PCI based network adapter, you should follow the directions in your computer's user manual for inserting PCI cards. Remove the cover, touch the case of the PC to eliminate static electricity, and then handle the network adapter. Install the network adapter in the proper slot. Close the cover and connect its power cord. For more detailed instructions on how to install and configure a network adapter, see *Appendix B, Installing Network Adapters*. Then complete the steps below.

   To install a PC Card (PCMCIA) based network adapter, you can just slide it into the slot of your computer. It should be automatically recognized and configured when you restart your computer.

   To install a USB based network adapter, you can just insert the appropriate USB connector first into the network adapter, and then into the USB jack of your computer. It should be automatically recognized and configured when you restart your computer.

2. Connect the installed network adapter to the cable modem using a blue RJ-45 Ethernet cable. If the cable modem is not powered, turn it on and wait a couple of minutes.

3. Turn your computer on. When your computer's operating system detects the network adapter, the computer will automatically install a software driver for it. This software allows the computer to operate the network hardware properly. If the operating system is too old or your adapter is too new, you need to help it install the software driver. In that case, insert the CD that comes with the network adapter into the computer. For more details, see the appropriate appendix that matches your Windows operating software (*Appendix C*, *Appendix D*, *Appendix E*, or *Appendix F*). Then complete the steps below.

4. Reboot the computer now. Next, configure the Internet software (called TCP/IP) for your computer to communicate properly with the Internet. This usually happens automatically. If you have an old version of Windows (e.g., Windows 98), you need to specify that you will use the TCP/IP protocol stack.

    Most recent versions of Windows (e.g., Windows XP) include a **New Connection Wizard** that guides you through the steps of setting up the network adapter and TCP/IP. For older version of Windows (e.g., Windows 98), the service provider may provide you a CD that installs the necessary software. For more details, see the appropriate appendix that matches your Windows operating software (*Appendix C*, *Appendix D*, *Appendix E*, or *Appendix F*). Then complete the steps below.

5. If your service provider supports dynamic IP address assignment, your computer's networking parameters need to be set to use the **DHCP** protocol. If your provider uses static IP address assignment, you need to set TCP/IP parameters yourself. For more details, see the appropriate appendix that matches your Windows operating software (*Appendix C*, *Appendix D*, *Appendix E*, or *Appendix F*). Then complete the steps below.

6. At this point, configure your email client if it is not already configured. You need your email name, email password and other pertinent information listed in the completed template in *Appendix A-2*. This entails setting parameters for the email client that you plan to use on this computer. See *Sections 3-6* and *10-7*.

Now test the computer and the cable modem connection. Make sure your browser can access the Internet and that your email service is working. Send an email message to yourself and see if you get it back at your computer. If all works well, you are ready to go to *Chapter 9* where we walk you through the installation of your home or office network. Otherwise, follow the troubleshooting steps in *Chapter 17*.

What you should read next

If you are	Read next
Someone wanting it "done for them"	Browse *Chapter 9, Setting Up Your Network*
A novice	*Chapter 9, Setting Up Your Network*
A typical user	*Chapter 9, Setting Up Your Network*
A power user	*Chapter 9, Setting Up Your Network*

8

Setting Up DSL Modem Service

This chapter provides the steps needed to get broadband service activated, if you are using a DSL modem.

8-1   Contacting a DSL provider

You need to sign up for the DSL modem service from your local DSL provider. When you do this, you find out details of the service, for example, when they will activate service, and whether the provider will install the DSL modem for you. **If this is an option, we strongly recommend that you let the DSL provider do this for you**. The installer will point out the phone line that supports DSL service, and ask you to indicate where you want the DSL modem situated.

The DSL modem connects to the Internet by a telephone wire, identical to the telephone wire used for connecting phones to the telephone network. It is best to locate the DSL modem near where you plan to locate your router and one of your computers, preferably one that is centrally located. We refer to this computer as the "first" computer. If you need to troubleshoot your network, having easy access to the router, DSL modem, and "first" computer is a plus.

Initially, the installer or you set up the DSL modem and the "first" computer to verify the broadband service. Later, you add the router and other computers to form your network.

The DSL modem connects to the DSL provider's network through the telephone wiring already installed in your home or office. Usually, a DSL connection can be made through any existing RJ-11 (normal telephone) jack. If the nearest RJ-11 jack is not easily accessible from where your DSL modem needs to be, the installer will need to install a new RJ-11 jack close to the DSL modem's location.

In most instances, DSL providers provide or rent the DSL modem to you. In addition, they provide without cost some number of additional elements called DSL micro-filters (*Figure 8-1*) needed to make the DSL modem and your telephones and fax machines operate properly. They may even connect the DSL modem to one of your computers. In some instances, you may have to purchase the Ethernet DSL modem.

8-1-1 Phone lines and DSL micro-filters

The DSL modem uses different frequency ranges to carry simultaneous telephone, fax, and data traffic. To avoid any interference between voice/fax and data transmission, **DSL micro-filters** must be connected to the RJ-11 jacks that connect to phones and/or fax machines in the home or office. The service provider usually provides some DSL micro-filters at no charge. If you have many telephones and fax machines, you may need to purchase more. Do not use a DSL micro-filter on the phone line that connects the DSL modem to the RJ-11 jack.

Figure 8-1: DSL micro-filter

Without DSL micro-filters, telephone or fax calls are degraded by static and hissing. A fax machine connected without a DSL micro-filter may lead to the fax call not connecting or operating at a lower speed. In addition, if DSL micro-filters are not used on every phone and fax machine, Internet connections and services will suffer interruptions. For the smooth functioning of the DSL modem and the other phone lines in the home or office, it is important to use DSL micro-filters.

8-1-2 Installer sets up the DSL modem

Here are the steps that you and the installer go through to set up the DSL modem and your "first" computer, usually the computer closest to the DSL modem.

You collect the information in the templates in *Appendix A-2* and *Appendix A-5* from the installer. You will need this later to configure your computers and your router.

1. The installer verifies that your computer already has a network adapter, or installs one in your computer.

    The DSL modem must have an RJ-45 Ethernet jack for your computer if you are to use it in your network. Most new DSL modems support RJ-45 and USB connections, but some models only support a USB connection. **Do not accept a modem that only has a USB connection.**

2. When a computer's operating system detects the network adapter, it will automatically install a software driver for the network adapter. This software allows this computer to operate the network hardware properly. If the computer does not have the needed driver, the installer inserts a CD that contains it.

3. The installer very likely reboots your computer, and configures the Internet software (called TCP/IP).

    Most recent versions of Windows (e.g., Windows XP) operating systems include a **New Connection Wizard** that guides the installer through the steps of setting up the network adapter and TCP/IP. For older versions of Windows (e.g., Windows 98), the installer may use a CD that installs the necessary software.

4. This is a good time to ask the installer about DSL micro-filters (see *Section 8-1-1*). The installer installs these on the jacks of your existing telephones and fax machines.

5. If your service provider requires the computer to run installation and registration software, it will be on the CD supplied by the DSL provider. The installer loads the needed programs from the CD and follows the steps outlined on the screen.

 6. If your service provider supports dynamic IP address assignment, the computer's networking parameters need to be set to use the **DHCP** protocol. If your provider uses static IP address assignment, make sure you recorded this information.

7. Ask the installer to set up your email account with the DSL service provider. This entails setting parameters for the email client that you plan on using. See *Sections 3-6* and *10-7*.

Installation should be complete. You should test the computer and the DSL modem connection before the installer leaves. Make sure your browser can access the Internet, and that your email service is working. Send an email message to yourself and see if you receive it. If all works well, you are ready to skip to *Chapter 9*, where we walk you through the installation of your home or office network.

8-1-3   You set up the modem

Obtain from the DSL provider or electronics store an approved DSL modem, an RJ-11 splitter, and the proper length of telephone wires with the RJ-11 connectors already installed to connect the DSL modem to the phone jack. An RJ-11 splitter (*Figure 8-2*) provides for an easy way to turn a single RJ-11 jack into two RJ-11 jacks. In most instances, DSL providers give you at no charge the DSL micro-filters needed to make DSL modem and phones operate properly.

 Remember to install a DSL micro-filter on every RJ-11 jack that connects to a phone, answering machine, and fax.

Figure 8-2: RJ-11 (phone) splitter

The DSL modem must support an RJ-45 Ethernet cable connection to your computer if you are to use it in your network. Most new DSL modems support RJ-45 and USB connections, but some models only support a USB connection. **Do not accept a modem that only has a USB connection.**

The easiest way to make the connection is to use an existing phone jack. Connect the RJ-11 splitter into the jack and use a length of telephone cable with the RJ-11 connectors to connect one jack of the splitter (A) to the DSL modem RJ-11 jack (B). In some instances, this arrangement may degrade performance of the DSL modem due to the wiring in the home or office. Try another phone jack and see if you get better performance. If that does not work, it is best to call your DSL provider and have them complete the installation for you.

The RJ-45 Ethernet cable connects to the DSL modem output Ethernet RJ-45 jack (C). Congratulations! You have now completed this phase of the installation!

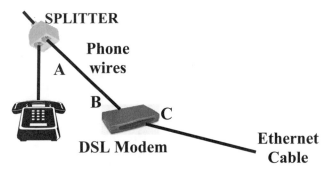

Figure 8-3: DSL modem and phones connected to the phone wiring

After you reach this part of the installation, activate the DSL modem by calling your service provider and find out when it will be available for service. Collect the information in the templates in *Appendix A-2 and Appendix A-5*. You will need this later to configure your computers and your router.

You must ask the service provider whether they support static or dynamic IP address assignment. If static, you must obtain from the provider the following information: your static IP address, your subnet mask, the IP address of the default gateway, and the IP address (or addresses) of the DNS.

Some service providers send you a CD to install special software for installation and registration, instead of giving you the information listed above. If the service provider sets up an account on your behalf then they will give you all the necessary information.

Here are the steps that you must go through to set up the DSL modem and your "first" computer, usually the computer closest to the DSL modem.

1. Verify that your computer already has a network adapter, or install one. Most recently manufactured computers come with a network adapter that accepts an RJ-45 Ethernet connection. If your computer does not have one of these adapters, you must install one. Refer to the flowchart in Figure 4-9 to guide your selection.

2. First, shut your computer down normally. If your computer has a network adapter, skip to the next step. Otherwise, unplug the computer's power cord.

    To install a PCI based network adapter, you should follow the directions in your computer's user manual for inserting PCI cards. Remove the cover, touch the case of the PC to eliminate static electricity, and then handle the network adapter card. Install the network adapter in the proper slot. Close the cover and connect its power cord. For more detailed instructions on how to install and configure a network adapter, see *Appendix B, Installing Network Adapters*. Then complete the steps below.

    To install a PC Card (PCMCIA) based network adapter, you can just slide it into the slot of your computer. It should be automatically recognized and configured when you restart your computer.

    To install a USB based network adapter, you can just insert the appropriate USB connector first into the network adapter, and then into the USB jack of your computer. It should be automatically recognized and configured when you restart your computer.

3. Connect the installed network adapter to the DSL Modem using a blue RJ-45 Ethernet cable. If the DSL modem is not powered, turn it on and wait a couple of minutes.

4. Turn your computer on. When your computer's operating system detects the network adapter, the computer will automatically install a software driver for it. This software allows this computer to operate the network hardware properly. If the operating system is too old or your adapter is too new, you need to help it install a software driver. In that case, insert the CD that comes with the network adapter into the computer. For more details, see the appropriate appendix that matches your Windows operating software (*Appendix C, Appendix D, Appendix E,* or *Appendix F*). Then complete the steps below.

5. Reboot the computer now. Next, you must configure the Internet software (called TCP/IP). This usually happens automatically. If you have an old version of Windows (e.g., Windows 98), you need to specify that you will use the TCP/IP protocol stack.

   Most recent versions of Windows (e.g., Windows XP) include a **New Connection Wizard** that guides you through the steps of setting up the network adapter and TCP/IP. For older versions of Windows (e.g., Windows 98), the service provider may provide you a CD that installs the necessary software. For more details, see the appropriate appendix that matches your Windows operating software (*Appendix C*, *Appendix D*, *Appendix E*, or *Appendix F*). Then complete the steps below.

6. This is a good time to install DSL micro-filters (see *Section 8-1-1*). You install these on your existing telephones and fax machines.

7. If your service provider supplies additional software on the CD for installation and registration, then run that CD and follow the steps outlined on the screen. During the installation process, you may also register your user name and password, and supply information to the service provider for billing purposes. We recommend that you have available a copy of your phone bill or a credit card for charging the DSL service monthly fees.

8. If your service provider supports dynamic IP address assignment, your TCP/IP parameters need to be set to use the **DHCP** protocol. If your provider uses static IP address assignment, you need to set TCP/IP parameters yourself. For more details, see the appropriate appendix that matches your Windows operating software (*Appendix C*, *Appendix D*, *Appendix E*, or *Appendix F*). Then complete the steps below.

9. At this point, configure your email client if it is not already configured. You need your email name, email password and other pertinent information listed in the completed template in *Appendix A-2*. This entails setting parameters of the email client that you plan to use on this computer. See *Sections 3-6* and *10-7*.

Now you should test the computer and the DSL modem connection. Make sure your browser can access the Internet, and that your email service is working. Send an email message to yourself and see if you get it back at your computer. If all works well, you are ready to proceed to the next chapter where we walk you through the installation of your home or office network. Otherwise, follow the troubleshooting steps in *Chapter 17*.

What you should read next

If you are	Read next
Someone wanting it "done for them"	Browse *Chapter 9, Setting Up Your Network*
A novice	*Chapter 9, Setting Up Your Network*
A typical user	*Chapter 9, Setting Up Your Network*
A power user	*Chapter 9, Setting Up Your Network*

Setting Up Your Network

9

At this point, you should have the cable or DSL modem working properly with the "first" computer. It is time to build your home or office network. Remember that most cable and DSL operators provide limited support for your network. Therefore, you may need to revert to the "first" computer configuration any time you need to deal with their customer support service centers to test the basic cable or DSL modem connection.

It is time to purchase the previously identified components for your network. Once you have the components, we steer you through the task of assembling them.

This chapter shows you how to install the network elements that comprise your mini-internet. The next chapter shows you how to connect and configure your computers.

If you are going to use wireless, you have much less to do in this chapter. We cover this case first, followed by two wired configurations.

Here are the steps you follow:

1. Purchase your components.

2. Shut down your computers, and then remove power from the computers and modem.

3. If needed, install network adapters in your computers.

4. Place your router in the intended location, and connect it to the modem.

5. If your network needs one or more switches, place them in their intended locations. Cable the switches to the router using red RJ-45 Ethernet cables.

6. Connect each wired computer to its appropriate switch or router with a blue RJ-45 Ethernet cable.

After this, you are ready to configure the router, computers, and any wireless network adapters. We show you how to do this in *Chapter 10*.

We provide a website that contains general information on this and associated topics. For more details, please use our website: www.BooksInAFlash.com.

9-1   Purchasing the items on your list

After completing the steps described in *Chapter 6*, you should have produced a detailed list of the items needed to create your network. At a minimum, the list includes a router (wired or wireless), but it may also include cables, switches, and network adapters.

If you used our template, you have a nicely organized list, suitable to take to any computer or electronics retailer.

9-2   Turn off your computers, printers, and modem

You are ready to begin actually installing your network. This will be much easier and safer if you have powered off these devices. You should shut down each computer; turn the power off to your printers and your cable or DSL modem. Some modems do not have power switches, so just pull the plug!

9-3   Installing network adapters

You need to install network adapters in the computers without one. We presume you will be installing at least one wired adapter. If that is not the case, see *Appendix I, Wireless Only Installation* for additional help. Then complete the steps below.

We describe the steps of installing PCI network adapters, PC Card (PCMCIA) adapters and USB adapters in *Appendix B, Installing Network Adapters*.

9-4   Connecting the router

The first step is to disconnect the RJ-45 cable connecting your cable or DSL modem to your "first" computer. After placing the router at the intended location, connect it to the modem using the gray RJ-45 Ethernet cable. Be careful as you "lay" the cable to make sure it cannot be tripped over or otherwise interfered with.

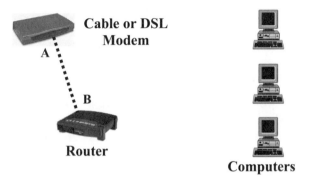

Figure 9-1: Connecting the modem to the router

The cable or DSL modem supports a port that accepts an RJ-45 Ethernet cable. The router has several jacks that accept an RJ-45 cable. There will be one, however, labeled **WAN**. That is the one used to connect to the modem. Using the specified gray cable, connect as described (i.e., connect **A** to **B** as above).

Please check to make sure that you have inserted the cable into the router's **WAN** jack. It will not work any other way.

9-5   Installing the remaining network components

Now, we describe how to install the remaining network components. You should match your network design with one of the standard configurations shown in *Table 9-1*.

Configuration	Described in Section
Wireless router	*Section 9-5-1*
Wired router, no switches	*Section 9-5-2*
Wired router, switches	*Section 9-5-3*

Table 9-1: Configuration instructions

9-5-1   Installing a wireless network

 If all of your computers will use wireless network adapters, you are finished with this stage of the installation. Before skipping to the next chapter, you may want to consider how to cable one of your computers to the router. Doing this will ease the task of configuring the router.

If one or more computers will use wired network adapters, you connect them to the router now. Follow the instruction in the next section to wire them safely and correctly.

9-5-2   Installing a simple wired network

A simple layout consists of a cable or DSL modem, a router and computers. Just a bit more complex are layouts that include switches. We describe how to set them up in *Section 9-5-3*.

It is time to connect your computers to your router. You need the blue RJ-45 Ethernet cables. For each computer, start at the router and connect one end of the cable into any open jack in the router. If your router has a jack labeled **UPLINK**, do not use this one! A computer connected to the **UPLINK** jack will not be able to connect to the Internet.

Carefully lay the cables, making sure that no one will trip over them. Connect the "other" end into the computer's network adapter. Repeat this for each computer.

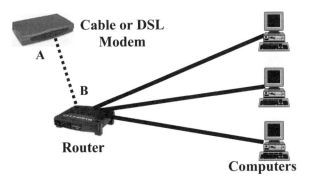

Figure 9-2: Router with computers connected to it

Once you have connected all the computers to the router, and the router to the modem, you are finished with this stage of the installation. Proceed to the next chapter to configure your network!

9-5-3   Installing a complex wired network

In this section, we describe a more elaborate arrangement including a router and switches. We follow a simple process, working our way from the router to the switches and finally to the computers.

We recommend a straightforward network design where the switches connect to computers and to the router (not to other switches). See *Figure 9-3*. For example, if there were a number of computers on the second floor, they should connect to a single switch. Then a single connection from the router to the second floor switch would support all these computers. It is perfectly all right to connect a computer directly to the router.

Start with the switch in your layout that is closest to the router. Place it where it belongs, and then connect it to an available jack on the router with a red RJ-45 Ethernet cable. Do not use a router jack labeled **Uplink** or **WAN**. After laying the cable, being careful to make sure that no one will trip on it or otherwise pull it, you must connect the other end of the red RJ-45 Ethernet to an **Uplink** jack on the switch. Some switches have only one **Uplink** jack, while others support **Uplink** on all jacks.

Repeat the steps in this section for any remaining switches in your network design.

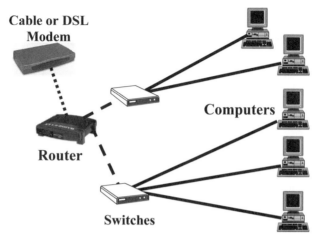

Figure 9-3: Network with router and switches

Now connect each computer to the appropriate switch using a blue RJ-45 Ethernet cable. For each computer, start at the switch and connect one end of the cable into any open jack in the switch **except into one labeled Uplink**. Do not use this jack!

Carefully lay the cables, making sure that no one will trip over or otherwise pull it. Connect the "other" end into the computer's network adapter. Repeat this for each computer.

Once all the computers are connected, you will end up with each computer connected to the router or to a switch, each switch connected to the router, and the router connected to the modem.

What you should read next

If you are	Read next
Someone wanting it "done for them"	Browse *Chapter 10, Connecting: Put it All Together*
A novice	*Chapter 10, Connecting: Put it All Together*
A typical user	*Chapter 10, Connecting: Put it All Together*
A power user	*Chapter 10, Connecting: Put it All Together*

10
Connecting: Put it All Together

Now it is time to configure the router and the computers of your network. When you are done with these steps, and after you have configured your email client, you will be able to surf, browse the Internet, and read and send email safely from each of your computers.

In the previous chapters, you installed and tested the cable or DSL modem, made sure there are network adapters in your computers, and placed and cabled the router, any switches, and computers. You are now ready to put it all together by configuring the router and computers. You are almost done!

Here are the steps you need to follow:

1. Turn the power off in your modem. Select a wired computer, preferably one that connects directly to the router, to be your "first" computer.

   If your network is wireless, we recommend that you connect a computer to the router using a RJ-45 Ethernet cable for this step. You can remove the cable and move the computer later. If this is not feasible, a wireless setup is possible, but you need to be extremely careful! We explain how to do this in *Appendix I, Wireless Only Installation*. Then complete the steps below.

2. Use this computer to set up and configure the router. First, start your browser and request the home page of your router. Next, configure the router with information you collected from the service provider, and if wireless, with security settings.

3. After setting up the "first" computer and the router, you are ready to open the connection to the Internet by turning on the modem, power cycling the router, and rebooting the computer.

4. If you did everything right, you should now be able to access the Internet from the "first" computer. Verify the correct functioning of the network and of the connection to the Internet. If functioning correctly, continue configuring the remaining computers in sequence.

If your network is not functioning correctly, see *Chapter 17, Consolidated Troubleshooting* for next steps.

10-1   Configuring the network settings

It is very likely that your "first" and other computers already have the proper network settings needed to connect to the Internet using a cable or DSL modem and a router. If this is not the case, you will detect this quickly in the next section, and we direct you to steps to correct the problem.

This is a good time to verify that you have turned the power off in your modem and turned the power on in your router.

10-2   Configuring the router

Now that you have your network installed, the next step is to configure the router. This allows the router to identify itself to your service provider's network, and allows it to begin routing IP packets between your computers and the Internet. In this arrangement, the router appears as a computer connected to the cable or DSL provider's network.

Start your browser to access the router's configuration page. The router you have installed conveniently responds to your browser as if it were a web server. This makes configuring it as simple as starting your Web browser (i.e., Microsoft Internet Explorer or Netscape Navigator) and asking it to retrieve the page accessed by the router's IP address.

 In the following examples, we show the windows and details from a Linksys® router. The particular router you are configuring may display slightly different windows. Use appropriate entries from *Table 10-1* to match your particular router. For example, the IP address for NETGEAR® routers is 192.168.0.1.

If you have a NETGEAR router, you can find the detailed steps in *Appendix H.*

Router Type	IP address	User Name	Initial Password	SSID (if wireless)
Linksys	192.168.1.1	(None, leave blank)	admin	linksys
NETGEAR	192.168.0.1	admin	1234	Wireless
DLink®	192.168.0.1	admin	(None)	default
SMC® (wired)	192.168.2.1	(None)	(None)	default
SMC (wireless)	192.168.123.254	(None)	admin	default

Table 10-1: Configuration information for your router

Enter the IP address of the router's home page (e.g., for the Linksys router you enter 192.168.1.1) into the address panel of your browser and hit the enter key.

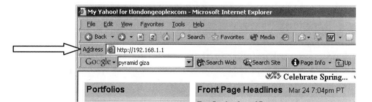

Figure 10-1: Requesting the router's home page

You should see a window similar to the one shown in *Figure 10-2*, asking you to enter a **User name** and a **Password**. This is the normal security check built into the router to prevent unauthorized access to the router's settings.

Figure 10-2: Router authentication window

If your browser does not pop up a similar window but displays a dialup connection or an error message, you need to take remedial action before you can proceed. Please read *Appendix G, Configuring Internet Options*. After you fix the settings of your Internet properties and browser settings, continue configuring your router. Enter the IP address of your router and see if you get a window similar to the one shown in *Figure 10-2*. Then complete the steps below.

The Linksys router is factory set with a password of **admin**. Leave the **User name** blank, enter this password, and click **OK**. (Don't worry about the password at this point. We show you how to change this in a moment.) You should see the router's home page displayed.

Figure 10-3 shows the home page of a wired Linksys router. For most networks, once you fill in a few entries on this page, your router will be ready to connect to the Internet.

Figure 10-4 shows the home page of a wireless Linksys router. Again, for most networks, once you fill in a few entries on this page, your router will be ready to connect to the Internet. However, if you have a wireless router, it is essential that you enter the proper security settings to avoid unrestricted wireless access to your network.

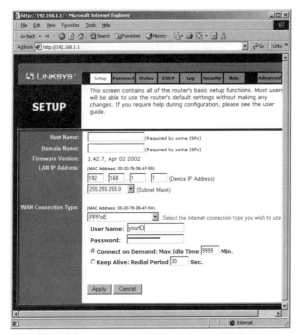

Figure 10-3: Wired router's home page

Figure 10-4: Wireless router's home page

At this point, you are ready to configure the router's network settings. This task varies in difficulty, depending on the type of configuration settings your cable or DSL provider expects. In the simplest case, the router needs almost no configuration. In the worst case, it requires a few lines of careful typing.

Depending on the details of your cable or DSL provider, you should read one of the following sections as described in *Table 10-2*. In addition, if you are configuring a wireless router, read *Section 10-2-4* afterwards.

Type of configuration	Described in Section
Your service provider uses DSL and PPPoE	*Section 10-2-1*
Your service provider uses "dynamic" settings	*Section 10-2-2*
Your service provider uses "static" settings	*Section 10-2-3*

Table 10-2: Configuring the router

10-2-1   Your service provider uses DSL and PPPoE

From the router's home page (*Figure 10-3* or *Figure 10-4*); select **PPPoE** as the **WAN Connection Type**. You should see a new home page with a few new entries that you fill in with information you collected in the template in *Appendix A-2*. In particular, you need to enter the DSL **User Name** and **Password** in the indicated entries. Also, set the **Connect on Demand: Max Idle Time** to 9999 minutes, to ensure that the IP connection is active most of the time. In the unlikely event that your service provider indicates that you need to set a few more options, such as **Host Name** or **Domain Name**, fill them in now. Remember to click the **Apply** button to activate these settings.

If you are using a wireless router, you should now read *Section 10-2-4*. Finally, the last step is to change the default password for the router. This is important to do. Otherwise, anyone with knowledge of the default router password will be able to reconfigure it. See *Section 10-3* below.

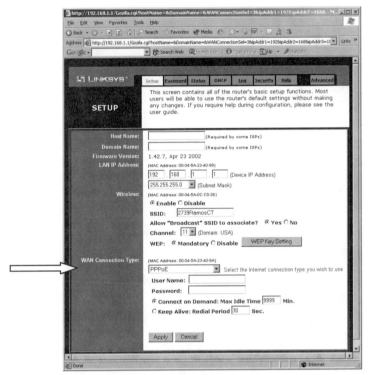

Figure 10-5: Setting PPPoE options

10-2-2   Your service provider uses "dynamic" settings

Your service automatically sets the IP address and other needed networking settings if it uses "dynamic" IP address. You need to make sure that the router has the **Obtain IP address automatically** option selected in its home page. If this option is not set, select this option now. In the unlikely event that your service provider indicates that you need to set a few more options, such as **Host Name** or **Domain Name**, fill them in now. Remember to click the **Apply** button to activate these settings.

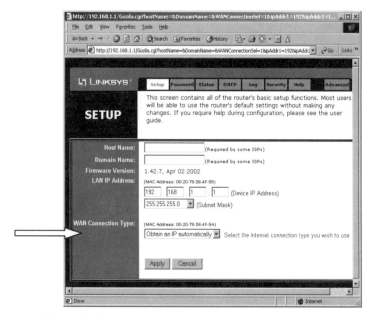

Figure 10-6: Router's home page – Obtain an IP automatically

If you are using a wireless router, you should now read *Section 10-2-4*. Finally, the last step is to change the default password for the router. This is important to do. Otherwise, anyone with knowledge of the default router password will be able to reconfigure it. See *Section 10-3* below.

10-2-3   Your service provider uses "static" settings

If your cable or DSL service provider assigns static IP addresses, you have a few more steps to complete the router's configuration. You already have all the needed information at hand, since you collected it from the service provider or installer to fill in the template in *Appendix A-2* (see *Table 10-3*).

The static IP address provided by the operator has the following form xxx.xxx.xxx.xxx (e.g. 66.77.65.231), that is, four numbers separated by periods. It is important to include all the periods and specify exactly the IP address specified by the cable or DSL provider. This IP address is your Wide Area Network (WAN) IP address, and each computer on the Internet uses it to talk to your computers.

Question to ask your provider		If yes, you need this information
If you are using DSL, does your provider use PPPoE?	Yes ☐ No ☐	User name: _____ DSL Password: _____
Does your provider require a specific hostname and domain name?	Yes ☐ No ☐	Hostname: _____ Domain name: _____
Has your provider given you a static IP address?	Yes ☐ No ☐	IP address: ____.____.____.____ Subnet Mask: ____.____.____.____ Gateway: ____.____.____.____ DNS server1: ____.____.____.____ DNS server2: ____.____.____.____
Does your provider support email?	Yes ☐ No ☐	Full email name: _____ POP3 server: _____ SMTP server: _____ Outgoing mail authentication? Yes ☐ No ☐ SSL for POP3? Yes ☐ No ☐ (if Yes, SSL port number: ____, e.g., 995) SSL for SMTP? Yes ☐ No ☐ (if Yes, SSL port number: ____, e.g., 465)

Table 10-3: Information you need from your service provider

In addition to the static IP address, the service provider gives you your **domain name**, (e.g., verizon.com or home.attbi.com), and three other settings. The first is your **subnet mask**. This is information that allows the various Internet routers to direct packets to and from you. It will probably be something like 255.255.255.0. The second is your **default gateway**. This is the IP address where your router sends all packets destined for the Internet (it is the "next router in the path"). The third are one or more IP addresses of the **DNS** your computer uses to translate IP names and URLs to IP addresses (see *Section 3-1-5*).

Make sure that you have correct values for these five parameters. If you do not have them, or you are not sure that the values you have are accurate, call your cable or DSL service provider. They can give you the information, usually over the telephone.

Use your browser to access the router's home page. Start by selecting the **Static IP** for the **WAN Connection Type** option. This should expand the page to include some new fields (see *Figure 10-7*). Enter the values for **Static IP Address**, **Subnet Mask IP Address**, **Default Gateway IP Address**, and **DNS** that you specified in your version of *Table 10-3*.

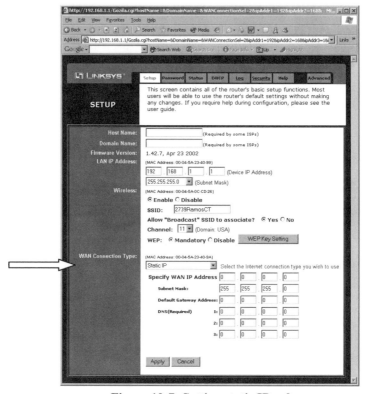

Figure 10-7: Setting static IP values

In the unlikely event that your service provider indicates that you need to set a few more options, such as **Host Name** or **Domain Name**, fill them in now. Remember to click the **Apply** button to activate these settings.

If you are using a wireless router, you should now read *Section 10-2-4*. Finally, the last step is to change the default password for the router. This is important to do. Otherwise, anyone with knowledge of the default router password will be able to reconfigure it. See *Section 10-3* below.

10-2-4   Wireless router

There are a few more steps to set up a wireless router. You need to make sure that the **wireless network name** (called the **SSID** or **ESSID** on different routers and network adapters; we use **SSID** when there is little chance of confusion) and **encryption settings** (called **WEP settings**) are set identically in your network adapters and in your router. The **SSID**, or wireless network name, applies only to the wireless components of your network and is different from the **Workgroup** name we described in *Chapter 3*.

In the following examples, we are showing the windows and details from a Linksys router. The particular router you are configuring may display slightly different windows. Use appropriate entries from *Table 10-1* to match your particular router. For example, the IP address for NETGEAR routers is `192.168.0.1`.

To start, you configure **SSID** and **WEP** values in the router. As above, connect to the router with your browser by specifying the router IP address as the destination address, e.g. `192.168.1.1`. **We strongly recommend that you perform these steps with a computer wired to the router, not one with a wireless connection to it**.

Notice the entries in *Figure 10-8* for **SSID** (where you enter your wireless network name) and **WEP** ("Wired Equivalent Privacy"). Your router has factory set defaults for these values (e.g., Linksys wireless routers use `linksys` for the SSID and disable WEP). There is another field, **Channel**, that sets the particular radio channel used for wireless communications, but you can leave this at the default value.

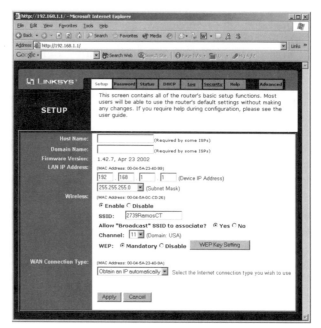

Figure 10-8: Wireless router's configuration page

You should change **SSID** and **WEP** values so your network will not be open to anyone nearby with a wireless network adapter. Otherwise, strangers will be able to see all your traffic and insert new traffic without your knowledge. **You must change these values to make your wireless network secure.**

First, enter a short and easy to remember name for your network. You may select the first eight to ten characters of your address, your last name, or anything. It should be easy for you to remember. Do not select names such as **Home**, **Office**, or **MyNetwork** that we suggested for **Workgroup** names.

Next, make sure to select the **Mandatory** button on the **WEP** line. You should print this page or write down the values you selected for **SSID**, (and **Channel** if you changed it) into the template in *Appendix A-5*. You need this information later to configure the wireless network adapters. Next, click the **WEP Key Setting** button (see *Figure 10-8*). This displays a window that allows you to configure the security settings.

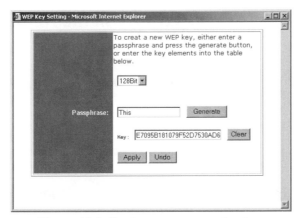

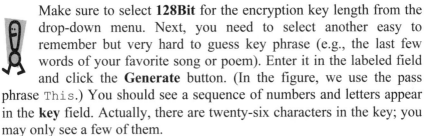

Figure 10-9: Setting your encryption key

Make sure to select **128Bit** for the encryption key length from the drop-down menu. Next, you need to select another easy to remember but very hard to guess key phrase (e.g., the last few words of your favorite song or poem). Enter it in the labeled field and click the **Generate** button. (In the figure, we use the pass phrase This.) You should see a sequence of numbers and letters appear in the **key** field. Actually, there are twenty-six characters in the key; you may only see a few of them.

If you have wireless network adapters from the same manufacturer as the router, all you need to do is remember the pass phrase. Otherwise, and more likely, you have to enter the actual twenty-six characters of the WEP key into each wireless network adapter manually. Very carefully, write the letters and numbers that comprise the key on a piece of paper. Double check to make sure you copied it correctly into the template in *Appendix A-5*

Make sure to click **Apply** both in this window as well as in the router's home page. In *Section 10-6-1*, you will use the software that manages the wireless network adapter to set its **network name** and **wireless encryption settings** to the identical values. If the settings on the router and the wireless network adapters do not agree, they will not "talk," and your computers will not be part of your network.

10-3   Setting the password on the router

At this point, it is a good idea to set the router's password to avoid unauthorized access to its configuration. Remember to keep all this information in a safe place for future reference.

You set the router's administrative password through its home page. Select the **Password** tab in the top left-center of the page.

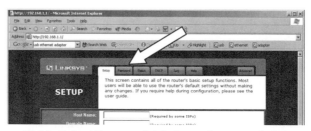

Figure 10-10: Select Password tab from the router's home page

The router's password window should appear.

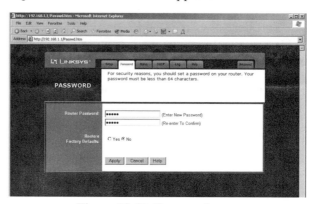

Figure 10-11: Password page

In the appropriate fields, you can enter your new password (twice to make sure you have typed it correctly!). Remember this password or pass phrase. You will need to enter it each time you want to access the router's configuration pages.

10-4   Restarting components

Now that you have correctly set up the "first" computer and router, it is time to reset and restart these items. Turn the power off to the router, and shut down the computer. Power on the cable/DSL modem, wait a few minutes, and then restore power to the router. This step is important to ensure that all these items have consistent configuration settings, and that each has the correct settings to work together smoothly. When you apply power to the router, it should come up ready to access the Internet through your cable or DSL modem and your service provider.

10-5   Testing network and Internet access

Boot up the "first" computer. If you have completed the steps in *Section 10-1* to *Section 10-4* correctly, you should have complete access to the Internet. A few simple tests should verify this.

Start your browser and surf to a few favorite locations. You should see web pages displayed quickly. For example, try `www.usps.gov`, `spaceflight.nasa.gov`, `www.state.nj.us`, or any three or four others that you choose. If you see web pages displayed on your screen, everything is set up correctly. Congratulations!

If you do not get web pages displayed, you should see *Chapter 17, Consolidated Troubleshooting* for next steps.

10-6   Configuring additional computers

You are almost done! What remains is to configure the other computers in sequence, similar to what you did for the "first" one. Boot up each wired computer in sequence, and test its access the Internet as in *Section 10-5*. Follow the troubleshooting hints in *Chapter 17* if you have any problems.

If you have wireless computers, you need to configure them now.

 Remember, you do not have to configure the router again. You only need to do this once.

10-6-1   Configuring wireless computers

You need to ensure that the computer's wireless network adapter and the wireless router use the same SSID (wireless network group name) and the same encryption settings. Otherwise, the wireless computer will not connect to your wireless network.

The details of setting these values depend on your wireless network adapter and the version of Windows on your computer.

You need to complete the following steps:

1. Retrieve the wireless settings for your router. These settings are the ones you wrote down in the template in *Appendix A-5*. You need the SSID, the WEP pass phrase and the WEP key. Be especially careful to have an exact copy of the 26-character WEP key.

2. Windows XP will automatically start a wireless manager for you to set identical values in the wireless network adapters. In Windows 2000, Windows ME, and Windows 98 install and use the vendor-provided software to complete this task.

3. Your wireless network adapter should now automatically "connect" to the router and establish a wireless connection. A few simple tests should verify this.

If your adapter does not function correctly, you should see *Chapter 17, Consolidated Troubleshooting* for next steps.

10-6-2　　Obtaining your router's wireless settings

When configuring the wireless router in *Section 10-2-4*, you noted the values selected for the SSID, the wireless channel (if you changed it), the WEP pass phrase, and the WEP key in the template in *Appendix A-5*. You need these to configure each wireless network adapter. If you cannot locate this information, you need to re-connect to the router again using a browser on a wired computer and copy the appropriate information from the router settings.

10-6-3　　Configuring wireless network adapter

The configuration process requires you to set identical values for SSID and WEP settings as your router. Unless the computer is running Windows XP, you need to install specialized software provided with the wireless network adapter. Finally, test the configuration to make sure you can access your network.

We detail in *Appendix D-2* the process of configuring needed settings for a particular network adapter (NETGEAR USB wireless network adapter model MA101) on a computer running Windows 2000. The process is similar for Windows ME and Windows 98 SE (Second Edition). However, Windows XP has built-in support for wireless network adapters. We show in *Appendix C-2* how to configure wireless network adapters in Windows XP. Then complete the steps below. You may find the details of other adapters and other versions of Windows on our website, www.BooksInAFlash.com.

10-6-4   Testing the wireless network adapter

Now that you have your wireless network adapter set up, test it. An easy test is to start your browser to access the router's configuration page. The router conveniently responds as if it were a web server from your browser.

 In the following examples, we are showing the windows and details from a Linksys router. The particular router you are configuring may display slightly different windows. Use appropriate entries from *Table 10-1* in *Section 10-2* to match your particular router. For example, the IP address for NETGEAR routers is 192.168.0.1.

Enter the IP address of the router's home page (e.g., for the Linksys router you enter 192.168.1.1) into the address panel of your browser and hit the enter key.

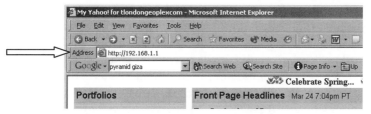

Figure 10-12: Requesting the router's home page

You should see a window similar to the one shown in *Figure 10-13*, asking you to enter a **User name** and a **Password**.

Figure 10-13: Router authentication window

 If your browser displays an error message, you need to take remedial action before you can proceed. Please check to make sure your wireless computer can "see" the router. We describe how to do this in *Appendix G-1*. Then complete the steps below.

10-7   Configuring email

Now that you have access to the Internet, you can configure your email client to receive and send email. Recall from *Section 3-6, Email – How does it work?* that there is a special software application, called an email client that connects to a special server, called an email server. Your broadband provider operates the email server, you must run a properly configured email client to receive and send email.

When you call to arrange for service from your service provider (or when the installer completes your installation), find out what email clients they support and the specific email settings needed to connect to their email server. You already have all the needed information, since you collected it from the service provider or installer to fill in the template in *Appendix A-2*. This template lists the POP3 and SMTP server information you need: the POP3 server allows you to receive your email, and the SMTP server allows you to send email. Besides the names of these servers, it is important to follow the instructions provided by your service provider to configure the email client. The instructions include information about your email user name, password, and security features, such as SSL, secure authentication, etc. If you have any problems with making your email work, please contact your service provider for help and troubleshooting.

10-8   Access to AOL and MSN

AOL and MSN offer reduced rates if you have your own connection to the Internet. They call this pricing plan BYOA (Bring Your Own Access). In fact, MSN currently does not charge if you use your own connection. If you use either AOL or MSN, read on.

 The windows and details we show are for the latest version of AOL and MSN. Your version of AOL or MSN may display slightly different windows.

10-8-1   AOL using broadband access

Double-click on the AOL icon to sign on to the AOL service. The usual sign on window will open up. (We show the AOL 6.0 sign on window; the sign on windows for AOL 5.0 and 7.0 are identical.)

Figure 10-14: AOL sign on window

In order to change the access settings to use your broadband access, click **SETUP**. A new window will appear:

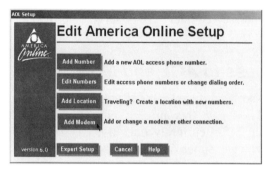

Figure 10-15: AOL setup window

Click **Add Modem** and it should automatically detect that you are using an Internet connection. AOL calls this a TCP/IP or ISP connection.

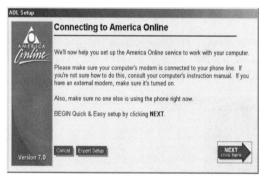

Figure 10-16: AOL help window for detecting connection options

Click **Next**, and let the software detect the connection options available on your computer.

Figure 10-17: Searching for connection options

Select the **Use TCP/IP or ISP (Internet Service Provider)** option, if it is not automatically selected.

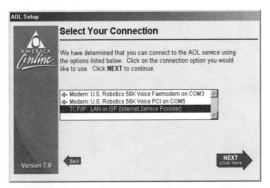

Figure 10-18: Select TCP/IP or ISP

Click **Next** to display the next window to confirm your choice. Now you are ready to use AOL using your broadband connection.

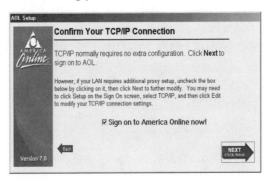

Figure 10-19: AOL confirmation window

You can lower AOL's monthly charges by signing up to their BYOA plan. However, BYOA may not lower your charges if you dial up AOL frequently while traveling by accessing AOL from a laptop.

If BYOA makes sense for you, change the billing plan after signing on to AOL by entering the keyword **Billing**. Then choose **AOL Billing Center→Change Your Billing Method or Price Plan**, click **Update Pricing Plan** and choose the **BYOA** pricing plan.

10-8-2   MSN using broadband access

Double-click on the MSN icon to sign on to the MSN service. The usual sign on window will open up.

Figure 10-20: MSN sign on window

Click **Connection Settings** (upper center) and a new window will display asking you to select the type of change you are making. Select **Change how you connect to the Internet** and click **Continue**.

Figure 10-21: MSN connection settings window

Select **Existing Internet Service Provider (ISP) or MSN Highspeed** and click **Continue**. You are now set to access MSN from your broadband connection.

Figure 10-22: MSN - selecting existing ISP access

11

Securing Your Network

11-1   Why it is dangerous out there?

People can see your home or office, they can identify the customary ways to enter or exit it, and they can easily test if doors and windows are locked. Highly motivated thieves can enter regardless of the state or condition of doors and windows. Once inside, a burglar can peruse your belongings, examine your documents, take, copy, or destroy items at will. They can be destructive: they can start fires, break plumbing; and they can leave booby traps or bombs. On the other hand, they can be quite subtle: they can leave no visible trace of their entry, perhaps, only copying information, leaving wiretaps or microphones behind.

In the same way, you are exposing your computers to potential probes, break-ins, and attacks when you have them connected to the Internet. It has a known and advertised "address" (your IP address). Legitimate traffic needs this address to find your computer. With a broadband connection, your computer can always be "online" or "always connected," you do not need to "dialup" or disconnect from the Internet.

As with your home or office, people other than your customers and friends become aware that your PC is "online." In fact, there are many people and groups probing and scanning for online computers. Some are legitimate, like search engines taking inventory of web-based information, while others have sinister motives, like stealing personal information stored on your computer. Once they know your computer's address, they can send arbitrary IP packets to it. This creates situations of risk for you and your computers. Make no mistake about it; *if you are connected, you are at risk*. You need to make sure that you lock your computer's "windows and doors," that you have a way of checking visitors' credentials, and that you make sure they do not leave behind unwanted items!

11-2   What is at risk?

Let us make no bones about it: you are at significant risk if you have a broadband connection and have forgone appropriate precautions. In the example of your home or office, your risks include not only each physical asset, but also the private information contained in your records and documents. A thief can steal unused checks or valid credit card numbers, or a diary that includes private information. They can use this information to masquerade as you or someone described in your documents. The thief could even leave something behind like a microphone, camera, or unlocked window that would provide access to your information later.

You should understand that, once inside your computer, an unscrupulous agent can effectively seize complete control over your assets, information, and valuable items.

If your computer has a broadband connection and you have not put in place prudent protections, here are just a few of the ways you have put yourself in harms way:

- All or any information on your computer(s) can be erased.

- Any information on your computer(s) can be "stolen" and posted in a public site.

- Any information on your computer(s) can be "stolen" and abused in secret.

- Computer resources, like disk space, CPU cycles, and network capacity, can be "hijacked" for someone else's use or for invading other computers. By the way, this is a convenient way for hackers to masquerade as you and hide their identity.

- Seeds of infection can be hidden within your computer(s) that "re-infect" yours and other computers at future dates.

Now that we have your attention, we describe simple and effective steps you can take to protect your computing and information assets.

11-3   The "bad guys" on the net

Let us first understand the likely risks from which you will need protection:

- Attacks initiated from unsolicited but normal-appearing Internet traffic directed at security flaws or weaknesses in your computer(s). Usually, such unsolicited traffic takes the form of probes into your network.

- Attacks embedded in requested and normal appearing Internet traffic that hide other functions; for example, an email download or a download advertised as a game. Such downloads can mask harmful or dangerous programs like viruses.

- Attacks that attempt to exploit weaknesses in your computer's operating environment, including the operating system, your web browser, your word processor, and your email client. Such attacks also can attempt to steal your computer passwords. Once a virus attacks your computer, it attempts to exploit your operating software weaknesses to harm your computer, someone else's computer, or steal your computer data or passwords.

Do not underestimate the persistence and creativity of hackers who would attempt to hijack your resources and information. You should assume that your computers will come under attack from the instant they are connected to the Internet. Some hackers are looking for software they can download free of charge and do not cause you any harm. Other hackers are out to cause extensive damage to your computer's disks and files. Since you cannot distinguish one hacker from another, you need to block all hackers from your computers.

Do not despair! To prevent or limit unwanted random attacks and probes from the Internet, you need something that filters Internet traffic for you. To limit your risk of downloading a "wolf in sheep's clothing," you need something that examines downloaded files for known "wolves," and a common sense set of rules to help you decide what to download and what to refuse. Finally, to reduce the likelihood that you will succumb to an attack exploiting a weakness in your Windows operating software, you need to keep your software up-to-date.

11-4   Simple pitfalls to avoid

Here is a list of pitfalls to avoid. To aid in understanding both the issues and the risks, we present this information in the form of a table drawing analogies to how you would set up and secure your home or office.

Your home or office	Your computer and network	Your solution	Understanding security concepts
Do not leave your doors and windows unlocked and unguarded.	Do not allow your computer(s) to have an unguarded connection to the Internet.	Install a NAT or firewall. See *Section 11-5.*	NAT or firewall. See *Chapter 14.*
Do not allow visitors unmonitored and unrestricted access to files and assets.	Do not allow arbitrary information to be copied from your systems.	Install a NAT or firewall. See *Section 11-5.*	NAT or firewall. See *Chapter 14.*
	Do not download files or programs from anywhere without checking for viruses ("wolves in sheep's clothing").	Install virus-scanning software. See *Section 11-6.*	Checking for viruses See *Chapter 15.*
Make sure visitors leave.	Do not download arbitrary files or programs without checking for viruses ("wolves in sheep's clothing").	Install virus-scanning software. See *Section 11-6.*	Checking for viruses See *Chapter 15.*
Change your locks if others may have keys.	Do not allow your systems programs to become out of date or obsolete.	You need to keep at least your Windows, Office and Internet Explorer software up to date! See *Section 11-10.*	

Table 11-1: Generic security pitfalls

11-5   What is a NAT or firewall?

There are two main types of security software used to monitor and guard connections to the Internet: NATs (Network Address Translators) and firewalls. Conceptually, both limit the Internet packets that flow between your computers and the Internet. They work differently.

A **NAT** is specialized software running on a computer or a router that sits between your network, which you trust, and the Internet, which you distrust. Computers on the trusted side usually do NOT have "real" IP addresses. Instead, they have locally unique but private IP addresses that are not meaningful in the Internet. Therefore, a NAT operates using two simple principles. First, it hides the identity of the computers it is protecting. Second, it only allows Internet conversations that start from a computer on the trusted side, not from computers on the Internet.

A **firewall** is specialized software running on a computer or a router that sits between your network, which it trusts, and the Internet, which it distrusts. Firewalls limit the Internet packets that flow pass it in either direction. They do this by maintaining two lists of rules, one that specifies allowable packets that can get through, the other that specifies disallowed packets that are not welcome. Most firewalls can also support the NAT function described above.

The good news is that most routers used for home and office networks come with the NAT functionality. Therefore, once you install a router you have the NAT protecting your network. You are done! For more understanding of NAT and firewall security concepts please see *Chapter 14, Protecting your Network.*

11-6   What is a virus scanner?

A **Virus scanner** is a program that checks your computer storage, including memory, hard disks, floppy disks, and CDs, for malicious software and matches patterns against a frequently updated database. The main varieties of malicious software are called viruses, Trojan horses, and worms; they all are commonly referred to as viruses. If a virus scanner detects a virus, it tries to "clean" or quarantine the virus.

We recommend that you set up the virus-scanning software to run continuously on all your computers, allowing it to check each new file as it is being prepared for storage. This provides you with unobtrusive but good protection from most virus attacks. The procedure we describe for setting up your virus-scanning software shows you how to configure it this way.

Additionally, since hackers are constantly at work, to be most protective, virus scanners need to have their database updated frequently. We recommend weekly updates of the virus database, with a more frequent schedule in the event of wide scale virus outbreaks.

11-7 Do you have virus-scanning software?

When you turn your computer on, it goes through a boot process that starts the Windows operating system. In addition, Windows starts a number of applications that need to be running all the time. One of those applications is virus-scanning software; it starts by performing a number of checks, including checking the computer's memory and startup files. Once the virus-scanning software has completed these initial checks, an icon or two appears in the system tray (the lower right corner of your screen). The icon allows you to change the settings or to start scanning your computer on demand. Since it needs to be active to monitor changes to all your files, the virus-scanning software also uses these icons to provide quick status.

After you have started your computer, please check to make sure that there is one icon in the system tray similar to any of the icons shown in *Figure 11-1*. If you place your cursor on this icon, it will highlight the specific application that it represents. If you see **VShield®** or **VirusScan® console** highlighted, you have **McAfee® VirusScan** software installed in your computer. If you see **Norton AntiVirus®** highlighted, you have Norton AntiVirus software installed in your computer. We cover both of these popular virus-scanning applications. We describe **McAfee VirusScan** in the following sections. We describe **Norton AntiVirus** in *Appendix J*.

Figure 11-1: System tray icons for virus scanners

If you do not see any virus-scanning software icons, please contact your computer supplier to find out if they installed virus-scanning software on your computer. Sometimes, installing new software may disable virus-scanning software unintentionally. If this is the case, make sure to check if the software is still on your computer by selecting

Start→Programs or **Start→All Programs**

and looking in the menu for a program from Symantec® (Norton) or Network Associates® (McAfee). Otherwise, reinstall the virus-scanning software.

If no virus-scanning software is installed or available, then **we strongly recommend that you purchase virus-scanning software and install it on your computer**.

We describe how to use your virus-scanning software. If you have Norton Antivirus running on your computer, please read *Appendix J*. If you have McAfee VirusScan, please continue reading *Section 11-8*.

 The windows and details we show are for the latest version of McAfee VirusScan. Your version of McAfee VirusScan may display slightly different windows.

11-8   Using McAfee VirusScan

You display the McAfee VirusScan control window by double-clicking on the McAfee icon in the system tray (the lower right area of your screen). It provides access to all VirusScan functions. This window indicates the version and date of your virus definition files, and the settings of a few important system parameters.

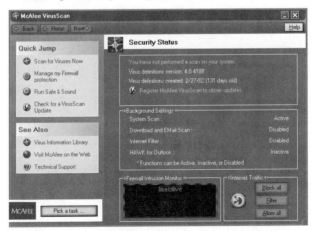

Figure 11-2: McAfee VirusScan control window

Clicking on **Scan for Viruses Now** displays a control panel window (*Figure 11-3*). Select the entry for **My Computer** and click **Scan** to cause VirusScan to scan all memory, hard drives, floppy drives, and CD drives on your computer.

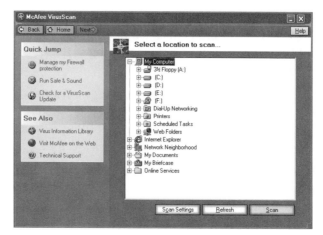

Figure 11-3: Scan "My Computer" for viruses

If you only want to scan your hard drive, typically the C drive, you highlight the C drive before clicking **Scan**.

Figure 11-4: Scan "C" drive for viruses

If VirusScan detects an infected file, it displays a window with options to clean or delete the file. If VirusScan cannot clean the file and you are not comfortable deleting files, you will need to seek professional help. At the completion of these scans, VirusScan shows results of the virus scanning activity in a report similar to the one shown in *Figure 11-5*.

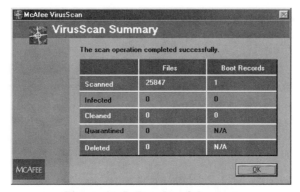

Figure 11-5: Results of the scan

11-8-1   Updating McAfee virus definition files

Displaying the VirusScan control window (*Figure 11-2*) displays when the virus definition files were last updated. You must update these files frequently to keep up with the new viruses.

You make VirusScan download new and improved virus files over the Internet from the main console window. Click on **Check for a VirusScan Update** link.

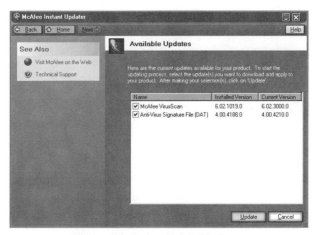

Figure 11-6: Available Updates

VirusScan contacts the McAfee website and identifies any appropriate updates. You should check all listed updates and click **Update**. You should see a status window indicating the progress of the download, and a window requesting you to reboot. After closing any other applications windows, click **OK** to restart your computer.

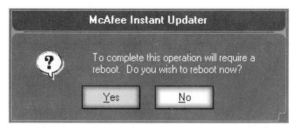

Figure 11-7: Update complete, time to reboot

You must update these files frequently to keep up with the new viruses. McAfee provides this service as part of the McAfee VirusScan Online package. **We strongly recommend that you register and subscribe to their automatic update service.**

11-8-2 Scanning an infected folder or file

If you suspect that a folder or file contains a virus, you should scan the folder or file with VirusScan. First, right-click on the folder or file. Within the menu, select **Scan for Viruses....**

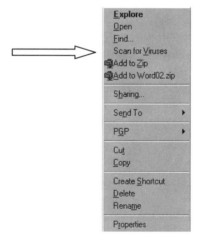

Figure 11-8: Menu to select scan of file or folder

VirusScan displays the window shown in *Figure 11-9* and quickly starts to scan the folder or file, finally producing a report similar to the one shown in *Figure 11-10.*

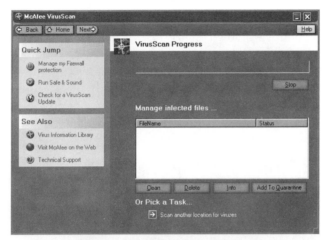

Figure 11-9: File or folder virus scan

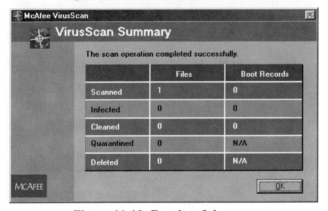

Figure 11-10: Results of the scan

If the folder or file is infected and McAfee VirusScan can remove the virus, you should allow it to do so. Otherwise, it is best to delete the folder or file and remove it from the Recycle Bin. Double-click **Recycle Bin** on your desktop and then click **Empty Recycle Bin**.

11-8-3   Enabling scanning for email

Email is now the most prevalent way of propagating viruses. To increase your protection, you should enable scanning of both incoming and outgoing email messages.

The windows below show how you can enable email scanning. From the VirusScan control window (*Figure 11-2*), click **Pick a Task** to bring up the selector window shown in *Figure 11-11*. Click the **Change my VirusScan settings** link to bring up the settings window shown in *Figure 11-12*. Click on the **Configure VShield background settings** to display the settings configuration window (*Figure 11-13*). Make sure you have the **Enable System Scanning** and the appropriate email-scanning box checked. Click on **Apply Settings**.

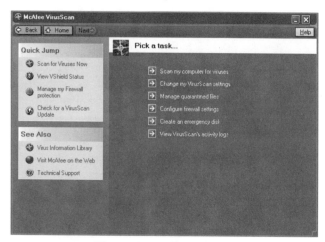

Figure 11-11: Pick a task

If your email software behaves strangely or you see many messages in your outbox that you did not send, probably an email message infected your computer with a virus. If that is the case, we recommend that you close your email program and disconnect your computer from the network as quickly as possible. Some viruses take control of your computer and you cannot shut down your email program. If this is the case, it is still best to isolate the computer by eliminating its connection to the network.

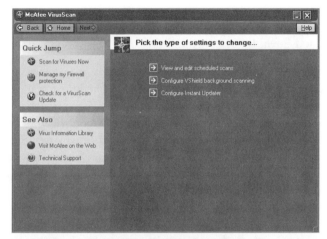

Figure 11-12: Select settings

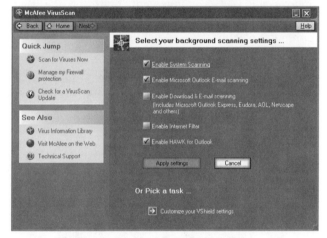

Figure 11-13: Set E-mail options

If your computer uses a wired connection, you should disconnect it by removing the blue RJ-45 Ethernet cable or the USB cable. If your computer uses a PC Card (PCMCIA) or USB network adapter, you should remove the card or device. If your computer connects using a wireless device, disable the network adapter. Refer to *Appendix B-5*. Once you disconnect your computer from the network, you can take your time to identify and fix the problem before it contaminates other computers.

11-8-4   Conducting periodic full system scans

It is a good idea to scan your computer for viruses regularly. We recommend that you follow the steps outlined in *Section 11-8* weekly.

McAfee VirusScan provides a mechanism to schedule automatic periodic scans of your computer. It eliminates the guesswork and helps keep your computer free of viruses. From the VirusScan control window (*Figure 11-2*), click the **Pick a task** button in the lower left corner. Return to the **Pick a task** window (*Figure 11-11*), click on **Change my VirusScan settings** to display the options selection window (*Figure 11-12*). Click on the **View and edit scheduled scans** link. From the **Manage a scheduled task** window (*Figure 11-14*), select the **Scan my computer** entry and click the **edit** button to display the **Task properties** window (*Figure 11-15*). Select the **Schedule** tab, and select the **Enable** and **Weekly** options and set a convenient time for the scan to start. Remember to click **OK** to accept the settings. We recommend that you scan your computer weekly.

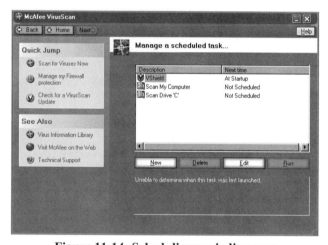

Figure 11-14: Scheduling periodic scans

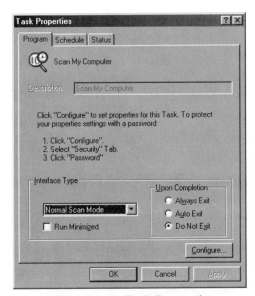

Figure 11-15: Task Properties

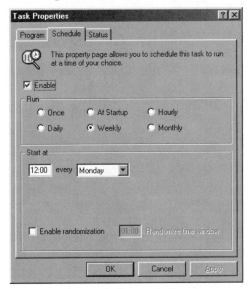

Figure 11-16: Set periodic scans

11-9   Setting or changing passwords

One easy method for someone to breach the security of your network is to guess or discover the passwords that you use. Therefore, you should change passwords regularly. Even though you have to change the passwords on your computers, your router, and your wireless components individually, it is worth investing the time and effort.

11-9-1   Computer passwords

Each version of Windows provides a slightly different way of changing passwords. Locate the section below that is appropriate to the version of the Windows operating system on your computer.

11-9-2   Windows XP and Windows 2000

1. After you have logged in to the system normally, simultaneously press and hold the **ALT**, **Ctrl**, and **Delete** keys.

2. Click the **Change Password** button.

3. Enter your current password and the new one. Click **OK**.

That is it! Remember to change it again at the appropriate interval. From now on, you will need to enter the new password each time you log in to the computer.

11-9-3   Windows ME and Windows 98

1. Select **Start→Settings→Control Panel** to open the **Control Panel**.

Figure 11-17: Windows 98 - Control Panel

2. Double-click on **Users** to produce the list of users authorized to use this computer. Select your user name by clicking on the appropriate name and click **Set Password**. That should display the **Change Windows Password** window.

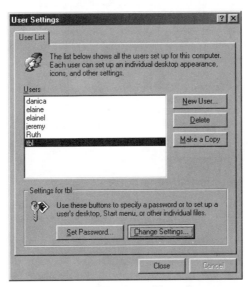

Figure 11-18: Windows 98 - select user

3. Enter the current and new password (twice!) in the appropriate fields. Click **OK**.

Figure 11-19: Windows 98 - set new password

That is it! Remember to change it again at the appropriate interval. From now on, you will need to enter the new password each time you log in to the computer.

11-9-4   Router password

Securing your router by changing its password regularly should limit unauthorized changes to its settings. Remember, your router is your first and primary line of security and defense. Keep it safe!

 We describe the steps for the Linksys router here. If you have a NETGEAR router, you can find the steps in *Appendix H-4*. For other make of routers, please refer to the documentation that came with the router.

Enter the IP address of the router's home page (e.g., 192.168.1.1) into the address panel of your browser and hit the enter key.

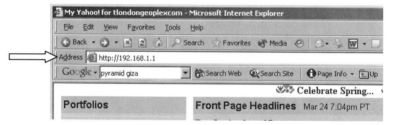

Figure 11-20: Requesting the router's home page

You should see the following window pop up, asking you to enter a **User name** and a **Password**.

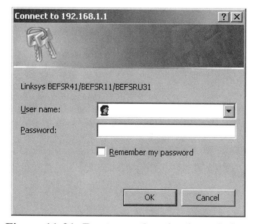

Figure 11-21: Router authentication window

Leave the **User name** blank, enter the current router password, and click **OK**. If you did not change the default password for the router as we recommended, the factory default is **admin**. You should see the router's home page displayed.

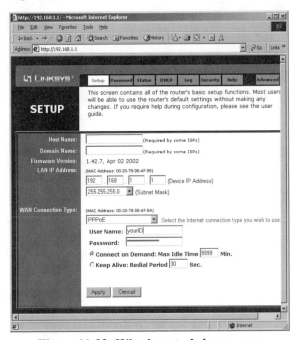

Figure 11-22: Wired router's home page

You set the router's password through its home page. Select the **Password** tab in the top left-center of the page.

Figure 11-23: Select Password tab

The router's password window should appear.

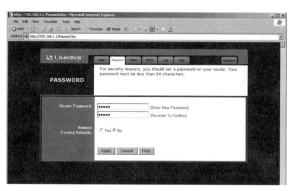

Figure 11-24: Password page

In the appropriate fields, you enter the new password (twice to make sure you have typed it correctly!). Remember this password or pass phrase. You will need to enter it each time you want to access the router's configuration pages. Click the **Apply** button.

That is it! Remember to change it again at the appropriate interval.

11-9-5   Wireless network passwords

Your wireless network and its components may be the weakest link in your network's fortress. You must apply more care and attention here than elsewhere. Make sure that you have enabled 128-bit encryption and make sure to change passwords regularly. Remember, you must change **WEP** settings in the wireless router and in each wireless network adapter.

11-9-6   Wireless router password

You set the **WEP** encryption settings in the router when you configured it in *Section 10-2-4*. Follow the steps in *Section 10-2-4* to change the **WEP** settings.

Remember, once you change the **WEP** settings in your router, your computers that use wireless network adapters will not be able to use the network until you update their settings as well. You should change their wireless encryption settings too.

11-9-7   Wireless network adapter settings

The steps you follow to set the **WEP** keys on your wireless network adapters depend on the version of Windows you are running and the peculiarities of each adapter. For computers running Windows XP, follow the directions given in *Appendix C-2*. For other computers, follow the directions given in *Appendix D-2-2*.

11-10 *Critical software updates*

Attacks from the Internet attempt to exploit weaknesses in your computer's software. Windows operating system software and other application software such as your email client, your word processor, and your browser could be targets. Software companies introduce software updates to guard against these attacks by plugging known holes. However, they discover new ones almost every day.

In most cases, you need to load a software update into each of your computers. The best way of doing this is to update your computer's software on a regular basis, say once a month, or more often if you discover major problems. Visit the website of the software companies whose applications you use to see if there are any critical software updates for you to download and install in your computers.

We showed you how to keep your virus-scanning application up to date (*Section 11-8-1* or *Appendix J-2*). Now, you need to update Windows, Office, and Internet Explorer as the most frequently used software in your computer.

New versions of Windows have a Windows Update entry in the Start menu that automatically takes you to the Microsoft update website. On this site, Microsoft lists updates for Windows and Internet Explorer. For Windows XP, select **Start→All Programs→Windows Update**, for other versions of Windows, select **Start→Windows Update**, and follow the steps outlined in the web page that appears. We suggest that you download and install all critical updates recommended by the software vendor. You can also find a link there for updates to your Office application (e.g., Word, Excel). In addition, visit the websites of the vendors of the software applications you use. Inspect the various downloads that are featured there.

12

Printer and File Sharing

In this chapter, we discuss the sharing of printers, folders, and files. If you do not need to share printers or folders and files, you can safely skip this chapter.

 We strongly recommend that you perform these steps only after you have installed and configured your router. Otherwise, you will expose your shared printers and folders to others on the Internet.

All current versions of the Windows operating system allow you to share the printers and folders on the computers in your network. This means that you can use printers and files on one computer from any other computer on your network. Sharing printers has the potential of reducing costs since you do not need to have a printer for each computer. Sharing folders increases reliability since you can easily keep backup copies of files on different computers. In addition, sharing folders increases efficiency since you can invoke applications from anywhere within your network.

In order to create your mini-internet and share resources, you need to name the computers and declare them as members of the same workgroup. Workgroups ease the task of administering shared folders and printers by establishing a common way of managing permissions. In this arrangement, **file servers** and **print servers**, computers that manage files and printers, can specify which users in a mini-internet can access which of their files and printers.

12-1 Entering the computer and workgroup names

We recommend setting up one workgroup for all the computers within your mini-internet. This means you need to select a name for the workgroup that is distinct from the names of your computers, and then "assign" each computer to that workgroup. Some examples of workgroup names include HOME, OFFICE, 127ParkAve, or Home-Group. For simplicity, we recommend using either HOME or Office.

If you have not done so already, this is a convenient time to set the name of the computer as well. Each computer must have a unique name to distinguish it from the others within the workgroup. We recommend you use the computer names you listed on the inventory sheet that you produced in *Section 6-1*.

 Windows workgroup names and computer names are not case sensitive. That means that HOME, Home, home, and hOmE represent the same workgroup name.

New versions of Windows have automatic wizards that do most of the work to set up a workgroup. The easiest way to get your computer named and added to a workgroup is to get the wizard running. You can do this in Windows XP by selecting **Start** and then clicking **My Computer**. Click the **My Network Places** link under **Other Places** to open the **My Network Places** folder.

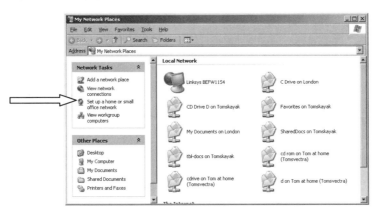

Figure 12-1: My Network Places folder

Select the link labeled **Setup a Home or Small Office Network** located under **Network Tasks** in Windows XP. This should get the network wizard going. Tell the wizard that you are setting up a home/office network behind a residential gateway. It should do the rest and prompt you for your computer and workgroup names.

If you do not have a network wizard or if you are using an older version of Windows (e.g., Windows 98, Windows ME, and Windows 2000), follow the steps below:

For Windows XP and 2000

1. If you are running Windows XP on your computer, select **Start→Control Panel→Performance and Maintenance→System**, if Windows 2000, select **Start→Settings→Control Panel** and double-click on the **System** icon. This will display the **Systems Properties** window (*Figure 12-2*).

2. There should be tab labeled **Computer Name** (Windows XP) or **Network Identification** (Windows 2000). Select it. You should see a window similar to the one in *Figure 12-2*.

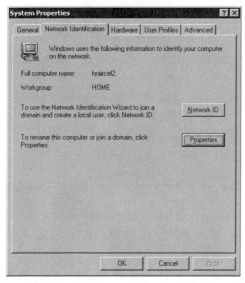

Figure 12-2: System properties for Windows 2000

3. Click on the **Properties** button for Windows 2000 (the **Change...** button for Windows XP) which will open the **Identification Changes** window in Windows 2000 (the **Computer Name Changes** window in Windows XP).

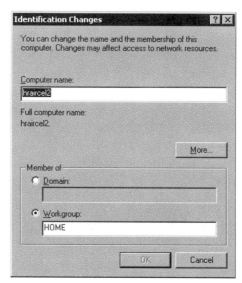

Figure 12-3: Change computer and workgroup names

4. Select the **Workgroup** option and enter the name of the workgroup in the entry field. In this example, we use HOME as the workgroup name. If appropriate, set the name of the computer in the indicated field.

5. Click **OK** on this and then the previous windows in order to make the changes permanent for this computer.

6. Your computer may tell you that it needs to reboot. If so, reboot now. You are done! You are ready to declare this computer part of your mini-internet.

For Windows ME and Windows 98

1. Select **Start→Settings→Control Panel**. This will open the **Control Panel** window (*Figure 12-4*). Double-click on the **Network** icon to display the **Network** window (*Figure 12-5*).

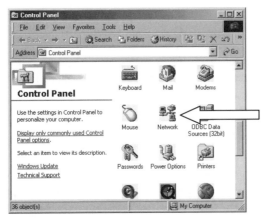

Figure 12-4: Control Panel - double-click on Network icon

 2. Select the **Identification** tab by clicking on it. In the **Workgroup** field, enter the workgroup name. We are using HOME as the workgroup name, but make sure to use the workgroup name you selected. If appropriate, enter the name of the computer in the indicated field.

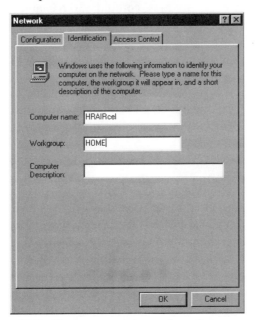

Figure 12-5: Change computer and workgroup names

3. Click **OK** on this and the previous windows to make the changes permanent for this computer.

4. Your computer may tell you that it needs to reboot. If so, reboot now. You are done! You are ready to declare this computer part of your mini-internet.

12-2   Sharing printers

You can share printers attached to any of the computers in your network. The computers with shared printers are called **print servers**. The print server must be powered and running when its shared printers are to be used. Computers that use shared printers are called **client computers**.

 We strongly recommend that you perform these steps only after you have installed and configured your router. Otherwise, you will expose your shared printers to others on the Internet.

Windows operating system software provides most of the "sharing" functionality. However, you must configure it to enable sharing.

In this arrangement, the full name of the printer will be

`\\print-server-name\shared-printer-name`

Therefore, it is important to know both the name given to the printer and the name of the print server. Do not forget to include the back slashes when entering the fully qualified name of the printer.

Here is what you do on each print server:

1. Determine the name of the print server.

2. Locate the icons of the printers you wish to share.

3. Set the sharing option for each shared printer.

4. Verify that the printer is shared.

Here is what you do on each client computer:

1. Locate the "Add Printers" icon.

2. Use the Add Printer Wizard.

3. Print a test page.

In the examples that follow, we use a printer named `hpdeskjet` connected to a print server called `HRAIRNT`. Remember to substitute your names in the appropriate places.

12-2-1   Configuring the print server for printer sharing

1. Determine the name of the print server.

    If you do not know the name of the printer's print server, here is a quick way to find out. On the print server

    For Windows XP and 2000

    If you are running Windows XP on your computer, select **Start→Control Panel→Performance and Maintenance→System**, if Windows 2000, select **Start→Settings→Control Panel** and double-click on the **System** icon. This will display the **Systems Properties** window (*Figure 12-2*).

    There should be a tab labeled **Computer Name** (Windows XP) or **Network Identification** (Windows 2000). Select it. You should see a window similar to the one in *Figure 12-2*.

    You can find the name of the print server displayed in the **Full computer name** field.

    For Windows ME and Windows 98

    Select **Start→Settings→Control Panel**. This will open the **Control Panel** window (*Figure 12-4*). Double-click on the **Network** icon to display the **Network** window (*Figure 12-5*).

    Select the **Identification** tab by clicking on it.

    You can find the name of the print server displayed in the **Computer name** field.

2. Locate the icons of the printers you wish to share.

    On the print server, select **Start→Settings→Printers** (on Windows XP, you should select **Start→Control Panel→Printers and Other**

Hardware→Printers and Faxes). This should open the **Printers** window (the **Printers and Faxes** window in Windows XP).

Figure 12-6: Printers window

You should see icons for each printer installed on this computer.

3. Set the sharing option for each shared printer.

    Move the cursor over the icon of the printer you wish to share and right-click on it. From the menu, select **Sharing...**

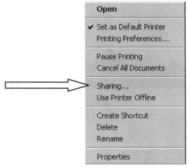

Figure 12-7: Selecting Sharing from menu

You should see the **Print Properties** window appear (*Figure 12-8*). Make sure to select the **Shared as** option, and enter `hpdeskjet` in the blank field. (The full name of this printer will be `\\HRAIRNT\hpdeskjet`. Remember to enter the name you wish to give your printer.) Click **OK**.

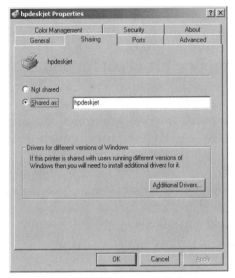

Figure 12-8: Sharing dialog

4.   Verify that the printer is shared.

The first check to see if you have correctly shared the printer is to examine the **Printers** window. Select **Start→Settings→Printers** (on Windows XP, select **Start→Control Panel→Printers and Other Hardware→Printers and Faxes)**. Within about 60 seconds, you should see the icon for this printer change.

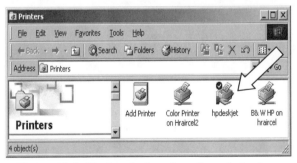

Figure 12-9: Notice the hand on the printer icon

Compare *Figure 12-6* with *Figure 12-9* Notice the hand icon, , that has been inserted into the printer icon indicating that the printer is now shared.

If you have more than one printer to share, now is a good time to repeat these steps for each of them.

12-2-2   Configuring the client for printer sharing

1. Locate the "Add Printers" icon.

   On each client computer, select **Start→Settings→Printers** (on Windows XP, select **Start→Control Panel→Printers and Other Hardware→Printers and Faxes)**. This should open the **Printers** window (the **Printers and Faxes** window in Windows XP).

Figure 12-10: Printers and Faxes window for Windows XP

For Windows 2000, Windows ME and Windows 98, the Printers window will look like *Figure 12-11*.

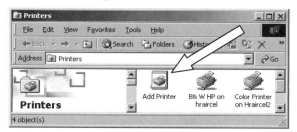

Figure 12-11: Printers window for Windows 2000, Windows ME, and Windows 98

This window displays icons for each printer installed on the computer. Also listed is an icon titled **Add a printer** that you use to adding more printers.

2. Use the Add Printer Wizard.

Double-click on **Add a printer**. You should get a window to start the wizard that sets up the printer. Please note that different versions of Windows may have variations in the wizard, however, they all follow a similar set of steps.

Figure 12-12: Add printer wizard

Click **Next**. The wizard walks you through all the steps needed to add this shared printer to the computer. When you see the screen asking you to select a local or network printer (*Figure 12-13*), select the **Network printer** option, and click **Next**. This displays a window asking you to locate the shared printer (*Figure 12-14*).

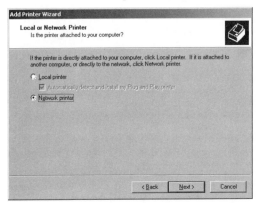

Figure 12-13: Selecting network printer

Now, select the **Type the printer name or click next to browse for a printer** option. In the **Name** field, enter the full name of the shared printer (e.g., \\HRAIRNT\\hpdeskjet) and click **Next**

display the **Default Printers** window (*Figure 12-15*).

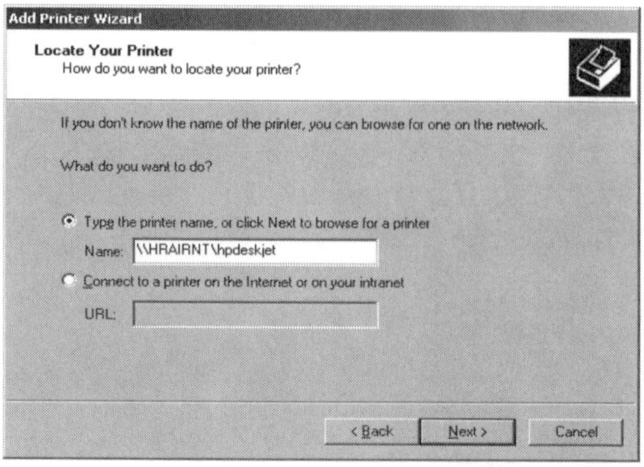

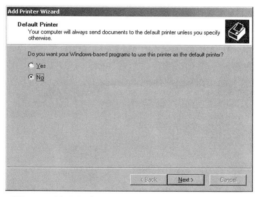

Figure 12-14: Select browse for a printer

Windows allows you to select a printer as the one you want to use most often (the **default printer**). If you want this printer to be the default printer for this computer, select **Yes**, otherwise select **No**. Then click **Next**.

Figure 12-15: Select default printer option

You are done! The only thing left to do is test the settings by printing a test page.

Figure 12-16: Finishing using the Add Printer Wizard

3. Print a test page.

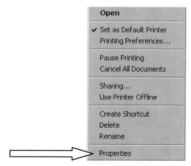

To verify that you have completed the setup correctly, you should now print a test page to the shared printer from the client computer. On the client computer, select **Start→Settings→Printers** (on Windows XP, select **Start→Control Panel→Printers and Other Hardware→Printers and Faxes**). This should open the **Printers** window (*Figure 12-6*).

Select the icon for the newly shared printer, and right-click on it. From the menu, select **Properties** (*Figure 12-17*). This will display the properties window for the printer (*Figure 12-18*).

Figure 12-17: Select properties of newly shared printer

In this window, select **Print Test Page**. You should see the test page status window appear on the screen (*Figure 12-18*), followed shortly by the test page printing on the printer.

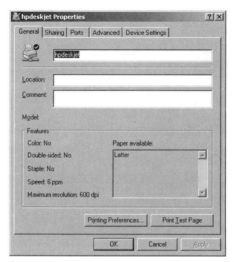

Figure 12-18: Printer properties window for Windows XP

For Windows 2000, Windows ME, and Windows 98, you should see a properties window similar to the one in *Figure 12-19*.

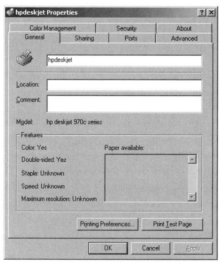

Figure 12-19: Printer properties window for Windows 2000, Windows ME, and Windows 98

If the page prints correctly on the shared printer, click **OK**. If not, follow the steps in *Chapter 17, Consolidated Troubleshooting* for next steps.

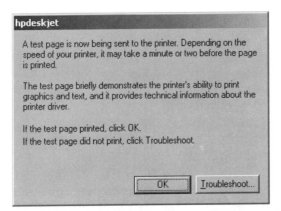

hpdeskjet

A test page is now being sent to the printer. Depending on the speed of your printer, it may take a minute or two before the page is printed.

The test page briefly demonstrates the printer's ability to print graphics and text, and it provides technical information about the printer driver.

If the test page printed, click OK.
If the test page did not print, click Troubleshoot.

OK   Troubleshoot...

Figure 12-20: Test page status. Press OK if successful

12-3   Sharing folders and files

In addition to sharing printers, you can share files, documents, and programs. In fact, you can set up your computers allowing general access and sharing of their files, supporting easier collaboration, better use of resources, and facilitating backup and recovery of key data.

We show you how to share folders on your network. The way you share a file is to share the folder it resides in. Of course, you need to make sure that the computers with the folders are powered and running when you want to use them.

 We strongly recommend that you perform these steps only after you have installed and configured your router. Otherwise, you will expose your shared folders to others on the Internet.

Windows provides most of the "sharing" functionality. However, you have to configure your system to permit sharing.

It is always a good idea to back up key files and folders to protect against loss due to hardware or software failures. It is best to make backup copies on another device and medium. Traditionally, one used tape storage devices for this purpose. More recently, burning compact disks to preserve key files and folders in case of catastrophic failures has become cost effective as well.

We show one way to use the network to backup folders on multiple computers. In case something goes wrong with a computer holding a key folder, there is quick and easy way of recovering it. Most computers now come with more than enough storage to accommodate backing up key folders in this way. Although not a complete replacement for archival backups, it suffices for many uses.

In this arrangement, the full name of the shared folder will be

```
\\file-server-name\shared-folder-name
```

Therefore, it is important to know both the name of the shared folder and the name of the file server. Do not forget to include the back slashes when entering the fully qualified name of the folder.

Here is what you do on each file server:

1. Determine the name of the file server.

2. Locate one of the icons of the folders you wish to share.

3. Set its sharing option.

4. Verify that the folder is shared.

 We recommend that you enable sharing only on those folders that contain files that you truly wish shared among all the users and computers in your mini-internet. Remember, once you enable sharing for a folder, users on the computers of your mini-internet can read and write all files in that folder. (It is possible to restrict more finely the access to your folders, but that is beyond the scope of this book.)

Here is what you do on each client computer:

1. Locate the "Add Network Place" wizard.

2. Use the **Add Network Place** wizard, and test access to the shared folder.

 We describe one example of sharing folders. In this example, we want to create a backup copy of a key data file named Financials on a computer named Tomskayak. To do this, we create a shared folder on a file server named London, and then copy the data file to the shared folder.

This is just one of many ways you can use shared folders, but should serve as a useful recipe. Remember to substitute the names of your computers, folders, and files in the appropriate places.

12-3-1　Configuring the file server for folder sharing

1. Determine the name of the file server.

    If you do not know the name of the folder's file server, we describe a quick way to find out the name of a computer in *Section 12-2-1*.

2. Locate one of the icons of the folders you wish to share.

    On the file server (in this example, we are using a file server called London), locate or create the folder you wish to share (in this example, we are using a folder called downloads). Next, you should start the Windows Explorer program.

    Windows XP:　　select
    　　　　Start→All Programs→Accessories→Windows Explorer

    Windows 2000:　select
    　　　　Start→Programs→Accessories→Windows Explorer

    Windows ME:　　select
    　　　　Start→Programs→Accessories→Windows Explorer

    Windows 98:　　　select
    　　　　Start→Programs→Windows Explorer

    It will display a system browser window similar to one in *Figure 12-21*.

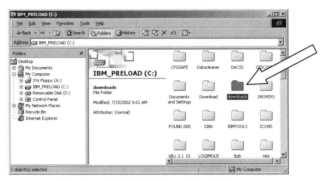

Figure 12-21: Windows Explorer

3. Set the sharing option.

Right-click on the `downloads` folder icon. From the menu, select **Sharing ...** (on Windows XP, select **Sharing and Security…**).

Figure 12-22: Selecting Sharing from menu

In the displayed window (*Figure 12-23*), select the **Share this folder** option, and enter into the **Share name** field the name by which this folder should be known, in this case, `downloads`. (In fact, the full name of the folder will be `\\London\downloads`). Other users will now be able to see and modify the contents of this folder. (On Windows XP, if you want users on other computers to be able to modify the files in this folder, you just need to check the box **Allow network users to change my files**.) Click **OK**.

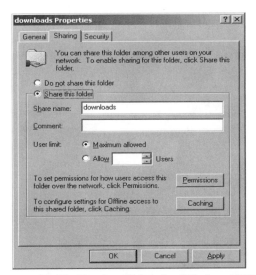

Figure 12-23: Sharing dialog for Windows 2000

The properties window for Windows ME and Windows 98 folders has only slight variations. We show the sharing dialog window displayed in Windows XP in *Figure 12-24*.

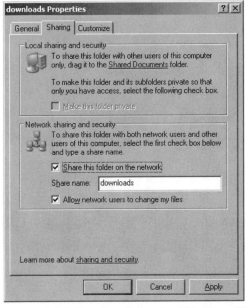

Figure 12-24: Sharing dialog for Windows XP

4. Verify the folder is shared.

Within about 60 seconds after you have set the sharing option, you should see the icon for the folder change.

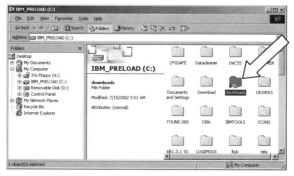

Figure 12-25: Notice the hand on the folder's icon

Compare *Figure 12-21* with *Figure 12-25*. Notice the hand icon, ![hand icon] , that has been inserted into the folder's icon indicating that the folder is now shared.

If you have more than one folder to share, now is a good time to repeat these steps for each of them.

12-3-2   Configuring the client computer for folder sharing

For Windows XP, Windows 2000 and Windows ME

1. Locate the "Add Network Place" wizard.

    Windows XP: select
    Start→My Computer and click **My Network Places** under **Other Places**. You will see the **Add a network place** icon located under **Network Tasks**.

    Windows 2000: double-click the **My Network Places** icon located on the desktop. You will see the **Add Network Place** icon.

    Windows ME: double-click the **Network Neighborhood** icon located on the desktop. You will see the **Add Network Place** icon.

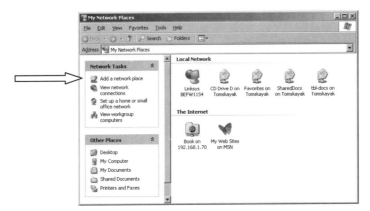

Figure 12-26: My Network Places window for Windows XP

2. Use the **Add Network Place** wizard, and test access to the shared folder.

    The steps are quite similar for Windows XP, Windows 2000, and Windows ME.

    Click the **Add a network place** link (or the **Add Network Place** icon for Windows 2000 and Windows ME) to start the **Add Network Place Wizard**. Press **Next** to get the wizard started.

Figure 12-27: Add Network Place Wizard

Select the **Choose another network location** option in the next window.

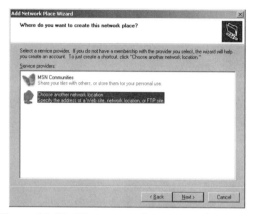

Figure 12-28: Choose another network location

This will display a window asking for the name of the shared folder. Enter the full name of the shared folder in the indicated location (for the example, it is `\\London\downloads`) and press **Next**.

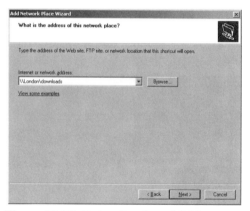

Figure 12-29: Enter the shared folder name

You can simply press **Next** to complete the configuration of the shared folder. The next step is to test accessing it.

In Windows XP, select the **Open the network place when I click finish** option. (In Windows 2000 and Windows ME, there is no such option.) When you click the **Finish** button, Windows opens an explorer window displaying the contents of the shared folder. If the explorer window pops up, you have done it all correctly. If not, you should see *Chapter 17, Consolidated Troubleshooting* for next steps.

Figure 12-30: Select Open the network place when I click Finish

For Windows 98

There is no **Add Network Place** icon in **Network Neighborhood** in Windows 98. Therefore, there is no facility to add and name an icon in the **Network Neighborhood** for shared folders.

You can access the shared folder by going to the **Network Neighborhood** icon on your desktop and clicking **Entire Network**. Then double-click on the workgroup and then the name of the file server for the shared folder. If the folder is visible on your screen that means your computer has access to that shared folder.

12-3-3   An example of folder sharing

 We show an example of backing up an Excel spreadsheet called `Financials` on `Tomskayak` into the folder on the file server called `London`.

Now, start Windows Explorer on the client computer:

Windows XP: select
     Start→All Programs→Accessories→Windows Explorer

Windows 2000:   select
     Start→Programs→Accessories→Windows Explorer

Windows ME: select
     Start→Programs→Accessories→Windows Explorer

Windows 98:   select
  Start→Programs→Windows Explorer

Locate the Excel worksheet called `Financials`, right-click on its icon, and within the drop-down menu select **Copy** (*Figure 12-31*). Then, using the same Windows Explorer window, locate the shared folder in the file server as described above and open it (*Figure 12-32*). Right-click within the window and from the drop-down menu select **Paste** to copy the file. You are done!

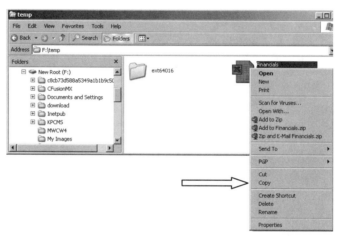

Figure 12-31: File to be backed up on client computer

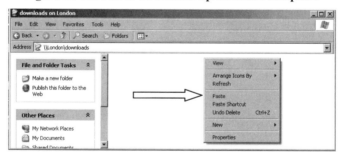

Figure 12-32: Paste file to copy to shared folder on file server

Part 3
Assistance and Concepts

13

Additional Assistance

We intend that this book be a complete and easy guide to getting your home or office network connected to the Internet. We believe that the book includes the right level of detail, correct and easy steps to follow, and a good set of recommendations.

In addition, we explain the concepts and technologies that make these products function the way they do. *Chapter 14, Protecting your Network* explains the concepts behind NATs and firewalls. *Chapter 15, Viruses and Malicious Software* describes how malicious software can damage your computers. *Chapter 16, Encryption and Authentication* explores how to protect your personal and private information on the Internet and how to guard against people masquerading as others.

However, we believe that ongoing support of your network will require more resources and updated information than we can supply with this static and fixed book. To that end, we have integrated the content of this book with a website. We believe we can thereby maintain the functionality, performance, and security of your network even as the industry introduces new products, services, and technologies.

We have set up the website, `www.BooksInAFlash.com`, into four main areas, each addressing the kinds of problems and issues you will need to deal with. Please visit this website and explore the possibilities.

The initial installation of a network will invariably be the most labor-intensive part. You may find that you require specialized assistance during this time.

	Standard Service	**Subscription Service**
Installation Support Services	Revisions and corrections to content, templates for network layouts, links to related sites	Advanced configurations & hardware, and in-depth troubleshooting questions and answers
Ongoing Support Services	Postings of Virus and security warnings, innovative products and technologies, etc.	Active virus and security contacts, recommended firmware and software upgrades, access to support experts, enhancements to networking technologies

Figure 13-1: Setup of `www.BooksInAFlash.com` website

Once your network is completely configured and implemented, you will need to redirect your attention to maintenance and support. If your environment is stable with few upgrades and changes, you will very likely have few installation related problems. You will need to address problems mainly in the maintenance and upkeep of the security safeguards that we strongly recommended that you implement. The website can serve as the focal point for your security maintenance operations.

If you choose to become a customer of our subscription service, we give you access to the broadest collection of tools, information and support we offer. We will keep this site updated with the latest recommendations and guidance, as well as provide step-by-step methods to introduce new products and technologies into your network.

If you choose not to become a customer of our subscription service, we will still provide you with access to information and help capabilities. We will provide revisions or fixes to the recommendations in the book based on the experience of our customers. You can be certain that you will be linking to the latest information.

14

Protecting your Network

In previous chapters, we stressed the routing and sharing functions of the router. In fact, the router does more than allow multiple computers to share a single broadband Internet connection. Built into it are security capabilities that significantly increase the safety of your network.

Although the technical implementation of these security capabilities is complex, the concepts behind them are relatively simple and straightforward. We explain them in this chapter by drawing analogies to the ways we secure our homes and offices.

14-1   Protecting your Internet connection

Figure 14-1: Unprotected home or office!

Imagine for a moment that you have the job of making sure that your home or office is not subject to either rampant theft or unwarranted intrusion. You would likely identify and secure the door. Placing a security guard at the door would ensure that you would be able to monitor people and packages both entering and exiting.

Figure 14-2: Office protected by security guard

We can draw an analogy to your home or office computers. You must ensure that your computers are not subject to rampant theft or unwarranted intrusion.

Figure 14-3: Unprotected computer

You need a computer version of a security guard that constantly monitors the communications between your computers and the Internet. Relax! There are available and inexpensive products you can use to guard your network. In fact, your router comes with security features and can sever as your security guard.

14-2   What are NATs and firewalls?

There are two main types of security guards used to monitor and guard connections to the Internet: NATs (Network Address Translators) and firewalls. Conceptually, both limit the Internet packets that flow between your computers and the Internet, but they work differently.

Let us return to the analogy of a security guard for a moment. In a small company, the guard would have a list of people allowed to enter and leave. In a larger company, people might have badges that indicate their status. As people pass, the guard checks each person and only allows entry to those authorized. In addition, the guard may have a list of known people to refuse entry (e.g., discharged employees) or known employees who are not allowed to leave with packages.

Let us examine the security operation in just a little bit more detail. Imagine a very secure facility or building. The building normally would have a single "area" where people and packages wishing to enter or leave would pass through. It would look like this:

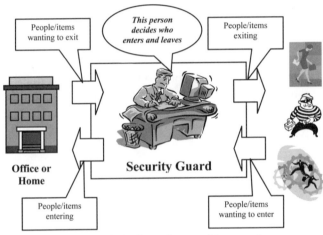

Figure 14-4: Generic security guard

In order to establish and maintain a secure environment for the facility, the security guard will need to examine each person or item entering or leaving. Suppose the guard recognizes a security issue, such as an employee attempting an unauthorized removal of equipment, or an unauthorized or suspicious person attempting to enter. The security guard must prevent this.

From time to time, it becomes necessary to change procedures. For example, the company may have terminated a consultant, contractor, or employee. To maintain security, the company needs to update the security guard's list. As the company's security needs change, it can focus attention in this one place.

The picture above actually describes both NATs and firewalls: the difference mostly being in the specific behavior of the security guard. Both NATs and firewalls can provide home and office security; there are differences in how they do it and what communications they allow. In the following sections, we first describe NATs and how they work, and then do the same for firewalls.

14-3   Overview of NATs

A NAT provides a simple way to provide network security. A **NAT** is specialized software running on a computer or a router that sits between your network, which it trusts, and the Internet, which it distrusts. Computers on the trusted side usually do NOT have "real" IP addresses. Instead, they have locally unique but private IP addresses that are not meaningful in the Internet.

A NAT operates using two simple principles. First, it hides the identity of the computers it is protecting. Second, it only allows communications that start from a computer on the trusted side, not from computers on the Internet.

Figure 14-5: Generic security guard

This means the security guard only allows letters or people into the building that are requested by someone in the building. To do this, people inside the building are assigned unique internal names not known or not meaningful outside (e.g., employee IDs), and can send whatever letters they choose. For each outgoing letter, the security guard logs the name of the sender, the name of the recipient, and the log sequence number for this letter. Before actually sending the letter, the security guard replaces the name and address in the return address with this letter's log sequence number and the address of the security guard.

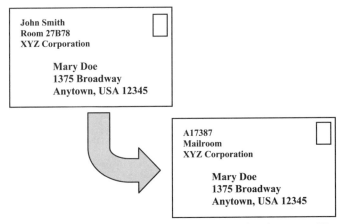

Figure 14-6: Guard replaces/hides source identity (return address)

For each incoming letter, the security guard checks the log to see if this is a valid response to a letter sent by an employee. The security guard does this by verifying that the recipient's name is a valid log sequence number and that the sender's name and address match the entries in the log. If so, the security guard restores the recipient's name and address, and forwards the letter on to the employee. If not, it rejects the letter.

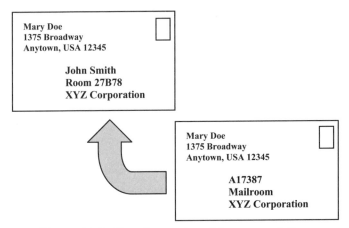

Figure 14-7: Guard accepts valid response letter

A random letter cannot make it through, since the name will be wrong or it will not be a valid response to a letter sent by an employee.

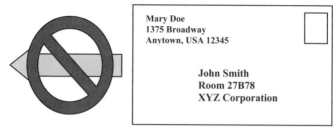

Figure 14-8: Guard rejects letter - "translated" name & address invalid

Figure 14-9: Guard rejects letter - sender not legitimate

14-4   How NATs work

NATs provides security by hiding the IP addresses of the computers on the trusted side from computers on the untrusted side. Different computers in your network will have unique private IP addresses. They can exchange packets and talk to each other without problems, but other computers outside the NAT cannot use these addresses to communicate to the computers in your network.

Conveniently, there are reserved IP addresses dedicated for this purpose. For example, addresses beginning with `192.168`, like `192.168.1.1` or `192.168.1.100` are commonly used for this purpose. Packets with one of these reserved destination addresses will not route properly on the Internet.

Consider an office with one or more computers and a NAT built into a router to protect its connection to the Internet (see *Figure 14-10*). One office computer has a private IP address of `192.168.1.100`. The router (and NAT) has IP address `215.37.32.203`. We examine what happens when the computer requests a web page from a server on the Internet with address `175.56.28.3`.

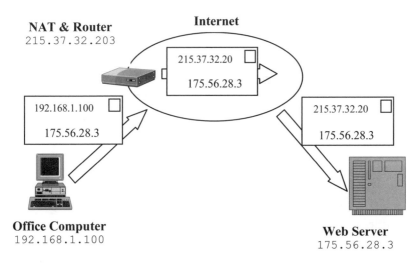

Figure 14-10: NATs – computer sends web request

Notice that the packet sent by the office computer contains its IP address, namely `192.168.1.100`. When the NAT receives this packet it must replace this private address with a public and routable return address, namely `215.37.32.203`, and then forward the packet on. At the same time, it remembers the IP address of the office computer and the IP address of the web server, remembering the pair (`192.168.1.100`, `175.56.28.3`).

When the web server receives the packet, it processes the request and generates information to return, namely the requested web page. It sends this information in a packet addressed to the return address in the first packet, namely `215.37.32.203`. When NAT receives this packet from the Internet it checks to see if it has remembered any pairs with the sender's IP address, namely `175.56.28.3`. Since it does in this case, it replaces the receiving address in the packet with the entry in the remembered pair, namely `192.168.1.100`.

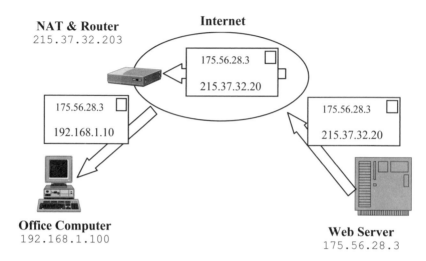

Figure 14-11: NAT - server responds

Behind the scenes, the NAT is doing a bit more than we just described. To see why, consider what would happen if a second office computer, say `192.168.1.101`, tried to browse the same web server at the same time. Each would send a packet to the web server, and the NAT would replace the private IP addresses for the two outgoing packets. It would also "remember" the pairs (`192.168.1.100`, `175.56.28.3`) and (`192.168.1.101, 175.56.28.3`).

Consider what happens when the NAT receives a response from the web server. The NAT will try to use the IP address of the sender, namely `175.56.28.3`, to find the proper remembered pair. However, it has two pairs with `175.56.28.3`. It cannot determine how to "undo the translation" to forward the packet.

When we send letters, it is not enough just to place the street address on the envelope. We need to include some additional and local delivery information, such as an apartment number, an office number, or a person's name to identify a specific recipient. By analogy, it is not enough to direct a packet just to an IP address. We need to indicate somehow the specific application. IP ports provide this added information.

IP ports are numbers chosen by servers and by your computer to identify each separate conversation or application. They are associated with every

IP address in each packet. Just as there are source and destination IP addresses, there are source and destination IP ports.

Some IP port numbers have standard uses. File transfers typically use IP port number 20 and web browsing typically uses IP port number 80 for the destination IP port. Your computer's software takes care of all of this for you behind the scenes.

To solve the above problem, when the NAT translates source IP addresses, it also translates source IP ports. Instead of remembering pairs, it remembers the IP ports as well. This way, when it receives an incoming packet, it matches the IP port as well as the IP address in the remembered list. The NAT hides the identity of the office computers by hiding their source IP addresses and IP ports.

To see how the NAT offers protection against random attacks, suppose a computer on the Internet tries to communicate with the computers behind the NAT. It will have several problems. First, what IP address does it use? Suppose it would like to reach the computer with private IP address 192.168.1.100. The private IP address is not a valid Internet address, so routers seeing such a packet will ignore it.

Suppose that the attacker instead tries to launch a packet with the NAT's public IP address as the destination. The NAT, when it receives this packet, will try to match it against its log of currently active communications initiated from computers behind the NAT. This packet will not match any such entry in the NAT's log. The NAT will prevent it from continuing.

14-5   What does a NAT protect?

Although its underlying mechanisms are simple, NATs provide excellent protection against various network based attacks from the Internet. However, they do not provide protection from security breaches originating from the trusted side. In home and office situations, this is frequently not a great problem, as the number of people and computers normally is limited, and major threats are seen to come from outside.

14-6   What is a firewall?

Firewalls limit the Internet packets that flow past it. They do this by maintaining two lists of rules, one that specifies allowable packets that can get through, the other that specifies disallowed packets that are not welcome. This is not as complicated as it sounds.

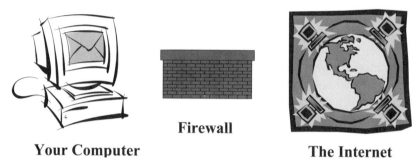

Firewall

Your Computer   **The Internet**

Figure 14-12: Computer Protected by Sentry

14-7   Overview of firewalls

Imagine we can describe a short list of rules that we would like the security guard to follow. Now the security guard can examine the content of letters and packages to help decide how to handle them. For example, we might provide the following list:

1. No one can remove company property from the facility without an appropriately signed "Package Removal Pass." The security guard must look inside packages to see if they contain company property.

2. Allow employees to enter or exit during normal working hours (8AM-6PM). Allow employees to enter or exit after 6PM only after they sign the log.

3. Do not allow entry to visitors on the "Do Not Allow to Enter" list.

4. Allow entry to other visitors during normal working hours only after an employee signs them in.

5. Allow approved contractors, such as cleaning and maintenance staff, to enter after 6PM, only after they sign the log.

6. Allow approved contractors to exit before midnight only after they sign the log.

7.　Otherwise, do not allow entry or exit.

Suppose we discover some additional activity that we want to restrict or prevent. Say we discover that some of our employees are sending documents to colleagues using CDs in letters. Notice that by simply adding the following rule to the security guard's list, we quickly prevent surreptitious CDs:

8.　Allow CDs to exit only if they are accompanied with an
　　appropriately signed "CD Shipment Pass"

What we have done is to create a "firewall" separating the inside of the facility and the rest of the world. Notice that the security guard does not do anything to modify the behavior of people or things on the outside.

14-8　How firewalls work

This is quite close to how an "Internet firewall" operates. Of course, instead of monitoring people and packages, it monitors Internet packets. However, it operates following the process described above. If you have put the proper rules in place, you can be sure that you have blocked unauthorized network traffic and the risks associated with unmonitored and unguarded Internet traffic.

A **firewall** is a specialized network element (or more precisely, specialized software running on a computer) that sits between two network regions: a tacitly trusted side, your network, and a tacitly mistrusted side, the Internet. The firewall waits for Internet packets to arrive, and when one does, it applies its rules. If its rules say "do not pass", then the packet is quietly dropped; if the rules say "let it pass", then the firewall allows the packet to proceed to the other side. In particular, note that firewalls examine and test packets both entering and exiting.

The rules allow the firewall to detect packets from particular sources (say, from `www.ImaThief.com`), for particular destinations (say, my email server), or using a specified protocol (e.g., email, web content, real-time voice). Packets can be explicitly passed or rejected. Here is an example of the kind of rules in a typical firewall:

Chain	input	(policy	ACCEPT):				
target	prot	opt	source	destination	ports		
ACCEPT	udp	------	anywhere	anywhere	any	->	ftp
ACCEPT	udp	------	anywhere	anywhere	any	->	ftp-data
ACCEPT	tcp	------	anywhere	anywhere	any	->	ftp-data
ACCEPT	tcp	------	anywhere	anywhere	any	->	ftp
ACCEPT	tcp	------	anywhere	anywhere	any	->	imaps
ACCEPT	udp	------	ns5.attbi.com	anywhere	domain	->	1025:65535
ACCEPT	udp	------	ns2.attbi.com	anywhere	domain	->	1025:65535
ACCEPT	udp	------	ns5.attbi.com	anywhere	domain	->	1025:65535
ACCEPT	udp	------	ns2.attbi.com	anywhere	domain	->	1025:65535
ACCEPT	tcp	-y----	anywhere	anywhere	any	->	http
ACCEPT	tcp	-y----	anywhere	anywhere	any	->	smtp
ACCEPT	tcp	-y----	anywhere	anywhere	any	->	pop3s
ACCEPT	tcp	-y----	anywhere	anywhere	any	->	ssh
ACCEPT	tcp	-y----	anywhere	anywhere	any	->	telnet
ACCEPT	udp	------	anywhere	anywhere	bootps:bootpc	->	bootps:bootpc
ACCEPT	udp	------	anywhere	anywhere	bootps:bootpc	->	bootps:bootpc
ACCEPT	all	------	anywhere	anywhere	n/a		
REJECT	tcp	-y----	anywhere	anywhere	any	->	0.710416667
REJECT	tcp	-y----	anywhere	anywhere	any	->	nfs
REJECT	udp	------	anywhere	anywhere	any	->	0.710416667
REJECT	udp	------	anywhere	anywhere	any	->	nfs
REJECT	tcp	-y----	anywhere	anywhere	any	->	x11:6009
REJECT	tcp	-y----	anywhere	anywhere	any	->	xfs
Chain	forward	(policy	ACCEPT):				
Chain	output	(policy	ACCEPT):				

Figure 14-13: Example firewall rules

Don't worry! You will not need to learn how to create and maintain such lists. Just be aware the task of managing and maintaining a real firewall can be quite complex and time consuming. Firewall rule sets need to be updated frequently to recognize new threats and new "bad guys" as they come along.

14-9   What does a firewall protect?

A properly configured firewall protects you against most probing attacks. A "bad guy" will not be able to get most traffic through to your computers. A firewall can also protect against some "copy out" attacks, where information is spirited away without your knowledge. This could take the form of copying files, software programs, or crucial information about you or your computer. This latter protection is however, incomplete. You will need additional techniques to protect against this threat.

Finally, a firewall can be useful to protect against so-called "denial of service" or "packet flood" attacks, where an attacker tries to disable your computers by flooding it with junk packets or requests. This is very similar to having your mailbox filled to the brim with junk mail. In a "denial of service" attack, your computer's access to the Internet will be impaired or completely clogged with junk packets.

14-10 Recommendations

We highly recommend the use of NATs for most small office and home situations. NATs come with the router you installed as part of your network. They are simple and adequate for most small office and home situations.

In large and complicated networks, we recommend you install a firewall. Firewalls provide some control over traffic that originates "behind" the firewall. NATs provide little or no such protection. If you are concerned about information leaking from your network, firewalls provide a better answer. Firewalls also give you the ability to filter selected sites and selected types of traffic. For example, if you need to restrict users from accessing certain sites, or from sending information to certain sites, firewalls are a better match.

14-11 Hard problems

Even after installing a NAT or firewall, you may experience very slow or no service when malicious perpetrators clog up the network you use to access the Internet or websites you browse.

In some instances, your computer or mini-internet may be the target of these malicious acts. If you followed our instructions in configuring your router, you will most likely avoid most of these problems. You need to be extra careful if you start changing settings on your router to open up various IP ports to outside traffic. Refer to *Section 14-4* for information on IP ports.

14-11-1 Denial of service attacks

If a computer, server, router, or switch connected to the Internet is flooded with junk packets; useful IP packets will have difficulty getting through. This happens because either the Internet connection cannot handle all the junk packets, or the computer, server, router, or switch expends all its useful energy throwing them away. Whether done intentionally or accidentally, access to the flooded component on the network is denied.

These attacks usually affect network servers and routers accessed and used by many individuals. A malicious attacker can leave others waiting for service by taking away most of these resources. For example, if an individual creates lots of fake traffic routed to a server, the network near it becomes congested and unable to support useful work. An analogy is a taxi cab "slowdown" that adds an inordinate amount of slow traffic between an entrance and exit on a heavily traveled highway, the whole length of the highway and neighboring highways become affected by the congestion. If you detect such a network attack, it is usually best to stop trying to access the internet until your ISP resolves the problem.

14-11-2 Port probes

Probes are used to monitor activities on the network. They are analogous to a meat thermometer that gives an indication of the inside temperature of a roast. Various kinds of probes perform a number of legitimate functions. For example, some probes help the management of networks or control messages.

Malicious attackers can use IP port probes to identify any open ports in your network to test them as an entry point for dastardly deeds. The type of router we recommend for your network does not expose ports to the Internet and therefore eliminates access to open ports. You can explicitly expose some IP ports in the router, for example, if you decide to run some kind of server. Be aware that doing so introduces a risk of attack. Tread carefully.

Viruses and Malicious Software

You need to understand that NATs and firewalls only protect you from intrusions from the Internet; they do not protect you if the activity originates from one of your own computers. In this chapter, we discuss measures that protect you from malicious software, commonly referred to as viruses.

15-1 Be aware of attacks

Unfortunately, there are many more lurking dangers for your computers and computer-based information than those eliminated by NATs and firewalls.

Let us go back to the analogy we used in *Chapter 14*. Assume we have a building with items needing protection, and employees who need to enter and exit each day. Assume we have a security guard to protect it against direct intrusions and employee thefts. Unfortunately, there are still many subtle, indirect attacks. Imagine that one of your employees receives a phone call from someone requesting confidential or proprietary information. In this kind of request, known as "social engineering," the attacker uses social customs, some specific company, or personal information to convince the employee that the request is legitimate. Imagine, for example, the following conversation:

> Attacker: Hello. This is John Smith. Am I talking to Bill Jones?
>
> Employee: Yes, this is Bill Jones. How can I help you?
>
> Attacker: Bill, I'm from the Finance group, and I've been asked to collect information regarding the upcoming

179

> *XYZ project. I have spoken with*
> *Steve Johnson in the Engineering*
> *group, and he says you've got all*
> *the financial details right there.*

Employee: *Yes, that's right.*

Attacker: *Well, first I could really use the*
> *bottom-line readout of the final*
> *bid amount. I'm hoping I can peruse*
> *the details later.*

Employee: *Well ….*

Attacker: *Let me start by giving you the*
> *address to forward copies to. OK?*

Employee: *OK. Let me get a pen.*

Disaster follows! This is not a farfetched situation. Social engineering is one of the more popular and effective techniques used to obtain information, access, and property. Potential losses due to people masquerading as someone else are unlimited.

There are similar dangers lurking on the Internet. Hidden in harmless looking software downloads, email attachments, spreadsheets and web pages are impending dangers. We describe some common ones and defenses against them.

15-2   Viruses, Trojan horses, and worms

There are several types of malicious software, but they share the goal of somehow inserting themselves on one of your computers, and then using its resources in some surreptitious manner. Effects can be harmless, for example, displaying a message on your screen once a day. They can be bothersome, for example, displaying a message on your screen once a minute. They can also be downright hostile for example, deleting important files from your disks.

Malicious software also vary in their manner of propagation; that is, how they get to your machine, and in their virulence; that is, how quickly they can spread from machine to machine. Especially bad ones have brought down large corporate networks and cost billions of dollars in lost revenue and recovery expenses. You cannot ignore malicious software!

We define the main types of malicious software. We give examples below. Although these malicious software agents usually gain access to your computer as part of a software download or email, your computer can also become infected by CDs or floppies inserted in your computer.

A **virus** is a computer program hidden in other computer programs and files that surreptitiously makes copies of itself. For example, a virus can infect a program such as Microsoft Word, causing a copy of the virus to attach itself to every Word document created by the infected computer. Viruses can reside in memory, on hard drives, CD, or floppy disks. Viruses frequently attach themselves to small and frequently used programs.

Viruses destructively change the functions of the computer or computer program that they infect. The application programs may act differently or strangely. They can damage or erase computer files or disks. Viruses can also be nondestructive. Regardless, you do not want them in your computers.

A **Trojan horse** is a program that hides its true purpose by masquerading as useful or helpful application. Once activated, its hidden function makes mischief. Unlike a virus, it does not propagate by copying or emailing itself to others. They propagate when users download them. Like viruses, Trojan horses can damage the infected computer and can be very destructive in nature.

Worms are programs that do not infect other files or programs, but spread by making copies of themselves, and by using the infected computer to send copies via the network to other computers. They infect other computers by using email and the network to copy themselves. Worms can damage the infected computer and can be quite destructive.

By these definitions, the social engineering example above is really a form of Trojan horse: the attacker is pretending to be a legitimate employee making a legitimate request for information. Chain letters are examples of a real life worms. Real life viruses are probably the best examples of viruses.

15-3   How malicious software propagates

As the name implies, these programs must attach themselves to your computer to do their dirty work. You might think that as long as you do not download any application programs, you will be safe. Unfortunately, the situation is much more complex, and hence more difficult to control.

Most commonly used Internet applications download files and information on their own. It is clear that you need to be careful when you download programs from Internet sites (you need to be careful even when you download from very trusted sites!). However, your email clients, your browsers, your word processors, spreadsheet programs, and even your instant messaging programs are all retrieving content from the Internet "under the covers."

Recently, some of the most virulent viruses and worms have spread by email using Microsoft Outlook and Microsoft Outlook Express as their method of infection. Since these "download requests" originate from a computer on the trusted side of the network, NATs and firewalls will not protect you. Something more is needed: something that not only looks at where IP packets are going or websites being visited, but what is being communicated. This "something" is a virus scanner, and no system should be without one.

It is not easy to list here the effects that viruses, Trojan horses, and worms can have on your systems because **there really is no limit to what they can do**. Do not be lulled into complacency; you may already be infected, and the damage already done. Imagine someone breaks into your home, and only takes some blank checks numbered well above the ones you are currently using. You might not discover the loss until you receive notice from your bank when your legitimate checks start bouncing!

There are too many active viruses, Trojan horses, and worms to list here. However, active downloads number above 60,000, with more created each week. Just keeping track of the new ones and producing the "vaccine" to recognize and remove them from computers is a major industry. You cannot do this on your own. You will need to engage one of the serious players of the industry to your side by purchasing and running one of the commercially available virus scanners (actually, they detect and clean viruses, Trojan horses, and worms) with their maintained and updated lists of active agents.

Although there are several good examples of scanners, we recommend that you purchase and install Norton AntiVirus or McAfee VirusScan. *Chapter 11, Securing Your Network* provides details on running a virus-scanning program.

15-4   Detecting and cleaning them

When a virus-scanning application detects a virus it usually displays a screen to notify you and takes appropriate action to eliminate the virus. In some instances, it may not be able to eliminate the virus, leaving it up to you to delete the infected file from your system.

The more difficult situation is when a virus, Trojan horse, or worm that is unknown to the virus-scanning software infects your computer. You need to be on guard for unusual behavior or activity on your computer. For example, when you see the "Send Items" email folder full of outgoing messages that you did not create, very likely a virus is creating and sending infected messages to people in your contact list or address book. In this case, it is best to shut your email application, disconnect your computer from the network, and eliminate the virus. In order to eliminate this virus, your virus-scanning application might need an updated virus definition file. You will have to obtain the update from the company that produced the virus scanner. Typically, you should download the update to a computer that is not infected with this virus.

Viruses that are more malicious delete your files and sometimes make your computer completely inoperable. In some extreme cases, you might need to reload your operating system from scratch. In such a case, you should seek professional help to clean your machine.

15-4-1   Preventing infection

The best prevention against common viruses is to know and trust the sender of the email or software. If you do not know who sent you an email message, do not open any attached files. Be especially wary of messages with tempting subject lines from unknown senders. Even if you know the sender, do not open the email if the subject line is suspicious or if the attachment appears to be a program file of some sort. You should be especially wary of attachments with filenames ending with ".exe," "bat," or ".com." Be careful, because a virus may have infected the sender's computer causing it to send these attachments.

Most people would not leave a door open allowing a stranger to enter their homes. Opening an attachment is equivalent to letting a strange program into your computer. Tempting or beguiling subject lines are a common way of leading you to open the attachments and invoke the mischievous program.

Another common technique is to embed the virus in some software package or electronic file given to you by others. Always check the source of the file and do not load any software not from a manufacturer that you know and trust.

If you cannot resist the temptation of opening the email or attachment, then before you actually open the file, at least scan it with your virus scanner updated with the most current virus definition files.

Finally, while surfing the Internet, whenever you find programs or updates to download, make sure you know where the program came from. If it comes from a trusted website associated with a reputable company, very likely you are at minimal risk. However, on the Internet there are few guarantees. Ask yourself "do I really need this program?" and "do I really know where it came from?" It is much better to be safe than infected!

15-4-2   Limitations and problems

If you take all these precautions, you stand a good chance of avoiding virus infections. However, remember that there are thousands of viruses, worms, and Trojan horses in existence, with others created all the time. You must update your virus scanner regularly and conscientiously.

The sad fact is that even with all of these precautions there is no guarantee that the virus-scanning software will be able to eliminate every new and unknown virus. If you are one of the unlucky ones infected by a new virus, you can minimize its impact and reduce your time to recovery by conscientiously backing up your critical files and folders. In extreme cases, you will need to seek professional help to clean your computer of the virus.

16

Encryption and Authentication

When you connect to the Internet, privacy of data and verification of user identity are two key issues. These problems are related. One way for someone to demonstrate their identity is for them to reveal some information that only they would know. One way to protect information from unauthorized use is to provide it only to someone having a need to know.

Encryption is the name given to techniques for scrambling and transforming information rendering it difficult to understand without knowing the reverse transformation, called **decryption**. Encryption methods are the lynchpin of your privacy on the Internet. In addition, since privacy and user identity are related, encryption is fundamental to how computers verify identity and authorize activities.

16-1   Brief tutorial

An ancient and still actively used method of protecting documents is to devise a rule, known only by the document's sender and recipient, for changing the letters and words contained in a document. The aim is to produce a "clouded" document that someone other than the recipient will think is gibberish. As an example, we demonstrate the use of one simple technique. Suppose we take each letter used in a message and replace it with the next letter in alphabet. The letter "**a**" becomes the letter "**b**," "**b**" becomes "**c**," "**l**" becomes "**m**," and so on. The only tricky part is what to do with the letter "**z**." We adopt the simple trick of replacing "**z**" with "**a**."

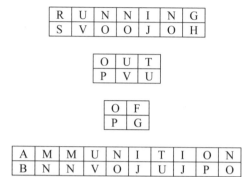

Figure 16-1: Replacing each letter with the next one

It is easy to see that we transform the message "**running out of ammunition**" to "**svoojoh pvu pg bnnvojujpo.**" It is also easy to see how someone spying on the message would be confused. The correct recipient, however, has the easy task of undoing the transformation by taking each letter, and replacing it with the letter prior to it.

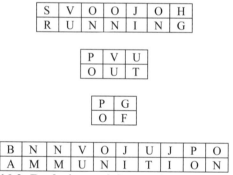

Figure 16-2: Replacing each letter with the previous one

16-2   Encryption and why it is useful

The encryption method in the example above requires little effort to decrypt, even without prior knowledge of the encryption process. So-called **strong encryption** techniques are those that are believed to be difficult to reverse without the knowledge of a specific secret **key**. The encryption methods used on the Internet generally are based on these strong encryption techniques. Consequently, our encrypted information should be as strong as the keys used.

A common way of providing encryption on the Web is a scheme known as **SSL** (Secure Socket Layer). In this scheme your computer and the Internet server handshake and securely agree on a secret key. Strong methods encrypt and decrypt the information. When SSL is active on your computer, you will see an icon of a closed lock on your browser (*Figure 16-3*) indicating that this feature is active, and hackers cannot view the information transmitted on the Internet.

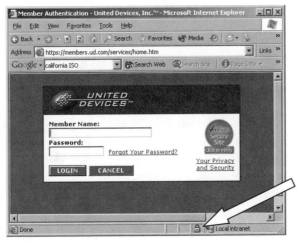

Figure 16-3: Notice lock in bottom right corner of Browser indicating secure transfers

Unlike our simple example, most up-to-date encryption methods make it very difficult to decrypt and encrypted messages without knowledge of the encryption key. In the case of some frequently used methods, it would take a supercomputer many centuries to figure out the original message. Hackers instead attempt to decrypt the message by trying commonly used keys.

16-2-1   Modern encryption techniques

Modern encryption techniques fall into two general categories: symmetric (or "one-key") and public key (or "two-key").

16-2-2   Symmetric encryption

Symmetric encryption methods use the same key to encrypt and decrypt messages. They are very useful when privacy is the main goal, and they are typically quite fast. In fact, strong symmetric methods are the backbone of modern electronic information security.

The strength of these systems is measured in key strength or key size. You may hear of 40-bit or 128-bit encryption. In general, the bigger the key size the more secure your data should be. Given the option, you should always choose the largest key size. In current practice, this usually means selecting 128-bit keys where you can. 40-, 56-, and even 64-bit keys are widely viewed as being easily broken by hackers. **We recommend you select at least 128-bit keys if asked.**

One place where you may have already seen such a choice is in the configuration of wireless networking components. We recommended that you select 128-bit WEP keys!

 If you select a key that someone might guess (e.g., the name of your significant other, your pet, your child or your car), you have provided yourself with **no** additional safety at all.

16-2-3   Public-key encryption

Public key encryption involves the use of two keys, one used by people that want to send you encrypted messages (called the public key), and one you use to decrypt those messages (called the private key). To communicate privately with someone, all you need do is pass your public key to him or her.

One way of thinking about public-key methods is to imagine that you have provided others with a large box of unlocked and identical locks for which only you have the key. Anyone wanting to "encrypt" a package to you would use one of these locks to lock the package. Once locked, only you would be able to "unlock" the package. Even the sender would not be able to open one of these locked packages, since only you have the key.

16-3 Authentication

It is frequently useful and necessary to be able to verify someone's identity. We typically accomplish this by demanding some form of credential such as a driver's license, a passport, or an affidavit from someone we know and trust. Analogously, we may need to determine the identity of the sender of information. For example, if you use the Internet to view your bank account, you want to be sure that the information originated from your bank.

Authentication is the process of validating the identity or source of an individual or information.

Windows uses a simple form of authentication when it demands a password to let you log in. Windows assumes that your password is a secret that only you know, and hence, being able to enter it is a form of credential.

Authentication is needed in other circumstances. When you connect securely to a web server when using SSL, your browser and the web server are exchanging forms of credentials and validating them so that your browser can be sure it is talking to the addressed server.

Suppose you want to determine if someone really is "Tom." Using the lock analogy from the previous section, you could write a message on a piece of paper and lock it in a package using one of "Tom's" locks. Asking a person to produce the content of your message would be a good test. If they were "Tom," then they would have a key to unlock one of the locks. Otherwise, an imposter's best tactic would be to guess, which would be easy to detect.

Real browsers and servers do not use something as simple as the process described above. However, they use something quite similar to this. Giving someone an encrypted message that only they can decrypt, and then asking them to produce the decrypted message is an excellent test of identity.

Wireless network adapters and wireless routers demonstrate a real use of authentication. In fact, you set identical encryption information in the router and in each network adapter to allow them to do this.

16-4   Password selection and management

You need to select passwords or passphrases with two apparently conflicting goals. First, they need to be easy for you to remember and enter. Second, they need to be difficult for anyone else to guess. We give you some suggestions on how to pick good ones.

Passwords should not be so obscure that you need to write them down. On the other hand, they should not be so short or obvious that anyone would guess them. There are folks out there with specialized password cracking programs that will guess obvious passwords.

 If you must write down your passwords, you should store this record in a place that is very secure. Finding passwords (or password hints) near the computer is a favorite tactic of hackers.

A short, but not exhaustive list of Don'ts:

- Do not use names, either first or last. Especially bad ones are the names of your dog, significant other, child, etc.

- Do not use the make or model of your favorite mode of conveyance. Especially bad are simple extensions of your car, e.g., "my Volvo."

- Do not use your license plate number.

- Do not use a dictionary word or sequence of dictionary words. Do not use words spelled backwards.

- Do not use the name of your computer, your phone number, your office number, your birth date, wedding anniversary, etc.

- Your social security number is a bad choice.

- Do not pick anything that is entirely in upper or lower case, or without punctuation characters.

Use your common sense! Here are some Do's:

1. Pick a sentence or a phrase (or lyric from a song or poem) that you will always remember (e.g., the song you first danced to). For example, "It was the best of times. It was the worst of times."

2. Misspell some of the words. For example, "It wuz the beast of timz. It was the wurst of dimes."

3. Replace some of the spaces with number or punctuation. For example, " It wuz!the beast7of,timz. It wuz;the7wurst of 10s". (Notice we replaced "dimes" with "10s").

4. Change some lower case letters to upper and/or visa versa. For example, "it wuz!tHe Beast7of,timZ. It wuz;the7wursT of 10s".

5. Shorten this to an appropriate length: the longer the better.

That should be enough. Type it a few times to make sure you can remember it WITHOUT writing it down!

There are other schemes, for example, dropping letters, selecting the first and last letters of the words of a phrase, that you can augment this process.

16-4-1   How often to change passwords

You should change your passwords and passphrases often. The longer you use a password, the greater the likelihood that you will make it available for someone to detect. Once that occurs, there is no security provided by them.

The passwords that require the most frequent updating are the password for the router, the password protecting your email account, and the key protecting your wireless components. They have the greatest likelihood of being detected outside your home or office. **We recommend that you change them every three to six months or as required. We recommend changing other passwords at least once a year.**

Part 4
Fixing Problems

17

Consolidated Troubleshooting

In this chapter, we present information that should allow you to troubleshoot any failure of your home or office network. If you can access our website, `www.BooksInAFlash.com`, you will find additional resources.

This chapter is organized along the lines of *Chapter 2, Insanely Quick Roadmap* in the beginning of the book. Search through the sections headings and item for the topic that best matches your circumstance.

17-1   Getting broadband service

1. **I do not know who offers broadband service to my home or office.**

   Read *Section 5-1*.

2. **I do not know whether to choose cable or DSL service.**

   Read *Section 5-2*.

3. **I only have one broadband service provider that can offer me service. What do I do?**

   Get service from that provider.

4. **There are no broadband providers in my area. What do I do?**

   Wait for a broadband service provider to enter your area.

17-2   Problems installing a modem

5. **I am not sure I know where to place the cable or DSL modem.**

   Several factors should help you decide. First, if you have a conveniently located main computer (more on that later), then you should try to install it there. Convenient means easily wired. It should be close to an existing or new phone jack (for DSL modem), or easily wired with coax cable (for cable modem). Outside walls are usually easier to wire than interior ones. Being close to, the service entry point is usually a plus.

Second, it usually makes sense to locate the modem close to your router. This way, you can see any indicator lights and manipulate the power cords on both easily.

Finally, if someone else is installing the modem, the installer will help you decide where it should be located.

6. **My cable or DSL modem is not really near any of my computers or router.**

This is not an enormous problem. You will just need a longer RJ-45 Ethernet cable to connect the modem to the router.

7. **My modem has indicator lights, but I do not see any of them lit or flashing.**

Check to see that your modem is connected to a powered electrical outlet. It is not a good idea to use an outlet that can be turned on or off from a light switch.

8. **My modem's indicator lights are flashing, but when I connect it to my computer, I cannot access the Internet.**

Make sure that you have configured the computer's network adapter to use the network settings provided by the service provider. See *Section 10-1*. If you need to, correctly configure the computer and restart it.

Check to see that you have correctly installed the RJ-45 Ethernet cable connecting the modem and the computer. Check to see that you are using a "straight through" RJ-45 cable (i.e., not a crossover cable). Also, check to make sure that you have connected the RJ-45 cable into the network adapter on the computer. (Other devices have RJ-45 like jacks, for example, an ISDN modem).

Finally, check to see if you can route packets onto the Internet by running a "ping test" (see *Appendix G-1*). If this is successful, it is likely that you have not properly configured your browser, or that you have not set the DNS (Domain Name Service) parameters properly, or the user name and DSL password used to authenticate for DSL service is incorrect. If the ping fails, you may have defective RJ-45 Ethernet cable connections, or you may not have set the default gateway parameter properly.

17-3   Problems with televisions and cable modem

9. **I no longer get pictures on my televisions. The pictures on my television are too grainy.**

If you had someone install the cable modem for you, have them come back to troubleshoot the problem.

If you installed the cable modem yourself, follow the coax cable back from the modem to the two-way splitter. Check the connection of all three cables. Defective connections lead to loss of signal power. Using a simple coax "barrel connector," eliminate the splitter, connect the two cables together, and test the televisions again. (A "barrel connector" connects two coax cable ends together.) You can purchase coax "barrel connectors" in any electronic store. If the picture improves, it is likely that the splitter weakened the signal for the television. Follow the steps in the next paragraph. If the picture does not improve, the connector on one or both of these cables may be defective. Fix it and try again. If the problem persists, try another splitter. Check other television sets in the home. If they produce sharp picture, check all the connectors back to that television. If you cannot fix the problem, it is time to contact your cable provider. They can send a worker to help fix the problem for a fee.

Sometimes the signal coming into your home is weak. Installing the two-way splitter may degrade the signal for your televisions and make the picture quality very poor. Check other television sets, if this is a problem on all your television sets, connect one of your TV sets at the point of entry to see if the signal is weak. If you find the signal is poor, contact your cable provider and ask them to come and check the signal quality. Make sure you tell them that you have broadband Internet service. If the signal is weak, they can usually upgrade the service coming into the home.

17-4   Problems with phones/faxes when using a DSL modem

10. My telephones or my fax no longer works.

If your provider installed your DSL modem, call them. It is likely that the installation broke a connection to your phones or fax machines. If you did the installation, check all of the connections. It is likely that one RJ-11 wire is not properly connected.

11. Every time someone sends me a fax or every time I use the phone, my Internet connection drops.

You have not installed micro-filters on every phone or fax. We really mean "each and every." Even one missing micro-filter can cause this problem.

17-5   Problems with layout and design

12. There is no esthetically pleasing way for me to generate a good layout for my network. I end up with wires all over the floor. My customers or my family will trip on them.

If you cannot discreetly run the cabling, you can either use wireless network adapters and routers, or obtain professional installation. Using wireless elements may increase the cost of your equipment, but it may be cheaper than a professional wired installation. You will end up with a simpler installation and one without wires on the floor. If you require a wired installation, having the home or office wired by an electrician will increase the cost, but you will avoid tripping over the wires.

13. I have only a few computers, but they are not close together. It looks like any layout will require excessively long cables.

If two or more computers are a bit close together, you can install a switch near these computers and connect them to the switch. That way, you can use one long cable to connect the router to the switch, and two shorter cables to connect the computers to the switch. Of course, you will have to buy a small switch, but these are quite inexpensive (around $20-$30). You will have to work out the economics to see which is less expensive.

If this solution does not suffice, you will have to opt for a wireless network. You will trade off a bit of increased expense for a lot of flexibility.

14. I have no good way of getting the cables between floors.

Call in a professional installer. Alternatively, you can opt for a wireless layout.

17-6   Problems with listing components

15. I do not know what components I need.

Appendix A contains templates to ease this step. You may want to copy the appropriate page for your use. Alternatively, you can visit our website, www.BooksInAFlash.com, for a table you can print that also will help you list the components. Please see *Chapter 6.*

Decide first whether you will need any wireless connections. This will lead you to list the needed wireless components (e.g., wireless network adapters, wireless router). Each wireless connection eliminates a wired connection.

If you need wired elements, you will need a wired router and a gray RJ-45 Ethernet cable long enough to connect the router to the modem. Each computer will need a network adapter (most have them already installed) and a blue RJ-45 Ethernet cable long enough to reach the router. If you need switches because your computers are far from the router, you will need a red RJ-45 cable to connect the switch to the router. Remember that your blue cables need to be long enough to reach the closest switch.

You will need a network adapter for each computer without an installed network adapter.

17-7   Problems obtaining components

16. Where do I purchase the needed components?

Visit our website, www.BooksInAFlash.com, for links to local and national retailers. You can also check the national chains that may be close to you: Frys, CompUSA, Best Buy, etc.

17. I do not know anything about computer networking. I am not comfortable making this purchase.

Take the complete "component list" that you prepared in *Chapter 6* to a retailer. The list will be complete. The only issues to discuss should be the specific router model and the price.

17-8   Problems with network adapters

17-8-1   Does my computer already have one?

18. I cannot tell if my computer already has a network adapter.

Almost every computer recently produced has a built-in network adapter.

Laptop: Examine the back and sides of the laptop and docking station to see if there is an RJ-45 jack (see what it looks like in *Figure 4-11*). Do not confuse an RJ-11 jack with a RJ-45 jack (see *Figure 4-12*). The RJ-11 jack has either two wires or four wires. The RJ-45 jack has eight wires. The RJ-45 jack is wider than the RJ-11 jack. If you can plug a telephone wire with no room to spare, it is a jack for a modem and not for a network adapter.

Desktop PC: Look for an RJ-45 jack in the back and follow the steps outlined above to make sure you use the right one.

In the Windows Operating System, you can also check the **Device Manager** to see if there is an entry in the network adapter section. You get to the **Device Manager** by selecting **Start→Settings→Control Panel** and double-clicking on the **System** icon (or selecting **Start→Control Panel→Performance and Maintenance→System** for Windows XP), selecting the **Hardware** tab and then clicking the **Device Manager** button.

The screen below shows the Device Manager and the expanded network adapter line. In this example, it shows the make and model of an Ethernet network adapter made by 3Com™ called EtherLink III™.

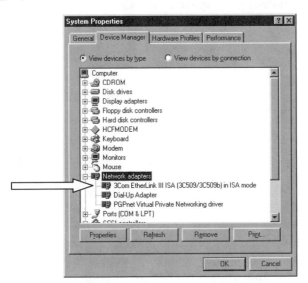

Figure 17-1: Device Manager with the expanded network adapter line

19. My computer seems to have no network adapter.

You will need to purchase and install one.

> **Laptop:** For a laptop, you will need to purchase a PC Card (PCMCIA) or a USB network adapter. Follow the directions in *Section 4-4* to make sure you get the proper network adapter for your computer. Install this in your laptop before proceeding.

> **Desktop PC:** You will need to purchase a PCI or USB network adapter. Follow the directions in *Section 4-4* to make sure you get the proper network adapter for your computer.

> Follow the steps in *Appendix B, Installing Network Adapters* for additional instructions.

17-8-2　How can I tell if the network adapter is working?

20. I have plugged the RJ-45 Ethernet cable into the network adapter, but it does not appear to work.

First, did you complete the steps to configure the network adapter? If not, follow the steps in *Section 10-1*.

If yes, did you reboot after connecting the cable? If not, it is possible that your computer did not get the correct network settings from the router and network. Reboot, and try again.

Check to see if you can run the "ping" test (see *Appendix G-1*). If you can, there is nothing wrong with your network adapter. You may need to check its settings. See *Appendix C* (Windows XP), *Appendix D* (Windows 2000), *Appendix E* (Windows ME), or *Appendix F* (Windows 98). If the network settings appear not to be valid, it is likely that either the cable is not correctly connected, or that the modem, router, and hubs/switches are not all powered. Check the cable, and check the modem, router, and any hubs/switches to ensure they are receiving power.

If all this is correct, it is possible that you have a malfunctioning network adapter. If you can, try replacing the network adapter with one you believe works. If the network adapter is defective, you need to replace it.

17-9　Problems with wireless network adapters

21. I have installed a wireless network adapter, but I cannot access the network.

After installing the wireless network adapter, you will need to configure it to allow it to talk to your wireless network. In particular, make sure you have set the proper network name (SSID) and encryption keys (WEP) to match the settings in your wireless router. In particular, we recommend that you use a computer that is wired to configure your router. See *Section 10-6-1*.

It is possible that the wireless signal is not reaching your network adapter with adequate strength. If you must use a wireless connection for this computer, and you have already tried moving the wireless router, you may need to install a wireless access point. Although beyond the scope of this book, you can find help on wireless access points on our website.

For a laptop: Move it within a foot or two of the router. If it works there, you need to adjust the antennas, the placement of the computer, or the placement of the wireless router

For a desktop: Try adjusting antennas and the location of the wireless router. Sometimes, wireless signals are very much dependent on the environmental conditions and building material used in your home. These factors may degrade the wireless signal to the extent of making it useless.

22. I have only intermittent access to the Internet.

You are most likely suffering from low signal strength or radio interference. Try adjusting the antennas, the placement of the computer, or the placement of the wireless router. You should try not to have large metal objects (e.g., refrigerators, air conditioners, etc.) that block the wireless signal.

It is also possible that other wireless devices could be causing interference. Many cordless telephones operate at the same wireless frequency as your network. It is also possible for microwave ovens and other wireless networks to cause difficulties.

17-10 Problems with cabling

23. I cannot plug my cables into the jacks on my modem, router, switches, or computers.

You have bought the wrong type of cables. You need to make sure that you have RJ-45 Ethernet cables.

24. I have a cable that is not the correct color.

You are OK, as long as the cable is not a crossover cable. Straight through cables (the usual ones) and crossover cables are NOT interchangeable. In this case, you will need to purchase the proper cable.

25. I have cables of the wrong length.

You have no problem if your cable is too long. You can just coil the extra cabling where you will not see it.

If the cabling is too short, it is possible to "join" them with an RJ-45 female-female adapter. We do NOT recommend this. Purchase the correct length of cable.

17-11 Problems with configuring computers

26. Windows tells me that I do not have permission to change the network settings of my computer.

On some versions of Windows, usually Windows XP and Windows 2000, you need to have "administrator" privileges to do this. The easiest way to get them is to log in as an "administrator." If you do not have administrator privileges then ask the administrator to change the network settings of your computer. If you cannot do this, you will need to obtain the administrator password from whoever knows it. If no one knows it, you will need to reinstall Windows.

27. Windows does not detect any network adapters.

If you have just installed a network adapter, you may need to install software drivers to the Windows operating system. Usually, Windows "detects" the new hardware and tries to install the correct software for you. It may ask you to insert the Windows CD, or you may need to insert a CD or floppy disk provided by the manufacturer of the network adapter. Failure to do this will cause Windows to disable the adapter.

17-11-1 Configuring the network settings

28. My computer came with a network adapter already installed. How do I configure its network settings?

You will find the steps to configure your network adapter and network settings in:

    Windows XP: See *Appendix C-1*.

Windows 2000:   See *Appendix D-1*.

Windows ME: See *Appendix E-1*.

Windows 98:   See *Appendix F-1*.

29. My system does not appear to have a Network Wizard. What do I do?

You will find the steps to configure the settings of your network adapter in.

Windows XP: See *Appendix C-1*.

Windows 2000:   See *Appendix D-1*.

Windows ME: See *Appendix E-1*.

Windows 98:   See *Appendix F-1*.

30. My network adapter is set up correctly to get network settings from the router, but it is not getting them.

Are you certain that you have correctly configured the network adapter? Please recheck. Remember you may need to reboot after changing settings.

Is the router powered? If you are using switches, are they powered?

Next, check the cabling to the router from this computer. Verify that you are not using a crossover cable and that you have not connected to the UPLINK or WAN ports on the router or switch.

If all your computers are having the same problem, it is likely that the router is not responding to DHCP requests. You need to reset the router and then reboot your computer. Read the router's documentation to see how to do this. Most routers have a **reset** button to restore it to the factory settings. Look for the reset button on the front or back panel of the router. Make sure that the router has power and then press and hold the reset button for about 10 seconds. The indicator lights on the router should flash and sequence a bit.

If after rebooting your computer, your network adapter still does not get settings from the router, it is possible that the router is malfunctioning. Try replacing it.

17-11-2 Configuring wireless network settings

31. My system does not appear to have a Network Wizard. What do I do?

You are going to have to configure the settings for your network adapter manually. Follow the steps outlined in *Item 29* above.

32. I have configured the wireless network adapter, but I still am not able to connect to the router or the Internet.

There are several possible problems: You may have a weak or nonexistent wireless signal, the **network name** in the network adapter and in the router may not match, or the **encryption settings** in the adapter and in the router may not match.

First, check the answer to *Item 21* to check out the adapter, antennas and signal. Most wireless network adapters come with client software that can monitor and display the actual signal strength. Check this to make sure it is adequate.

If that does not solve the problem, verify that the wireless **network name** and **WEP encryption settings** in the router and in your network adapter match. Follow the steps in *Section 10-2-4* to retrieve the router's settings. If you have no other computer that can connect to the router, you will need to "hard-wire" one with an RJ-45 Ethernet cable.

Once you have retrieved and/or set the router settings, use the software that manages the wireless network adapter to set the identical wireless **network name** and **WEP encryption settings**. See *Appendix C-2* (Windows XP), *Appendix D-2-2* (Windows 2000, Windows ME, and Windows 98).

17-11-3 Setting workgroup names

33. I cannot set the workgroup name.

If your computer is running Windows 2000 or Windows XP, you should first check to make sure that you have **administrator** privileges. If not, you should log off, then log in as administrator, and try setting the workgroup name again.

Windows XP: See *Appendix C-1.*

Windows 2000:   See *Appendix D-1.*

Windows ME: See *Appendix E-1.*

Windows 98:   See *Appendix F-1.*

If you still cannot set the workgroup name, very likely you will need to install the networking capabilities that support sharing of files and printers into your operating system.

a) **Windows XP**:
Select **Start→Control Panel→Network and Internet Connections→Network Connections**.

Windows 2000:
Select **Start→Settings→Control Panel** and double-click on the **Network and Dial-up Connections** icon.

Windows ME or Windows 98:
Select **Start→Settings→Control Panel** and double-click on the **Network** icon.

b) Right-click on the network adapter and select **Properties** from the menu. Check to see that **Clients for Microsoft Network** and **File and Printer Sharing for Microsoft** are included in the list. If not, click **Install**, select **Client** and click **Add**. Select these two capabilities and click **OK**.

c) The computer may ask you to put the Windows Operating System CD in your computer to add these components.

17-12 Problems configuring the router

34. I cannot use the browser to access the router's home page, but I can access the Internet.

a) Check the IP address you are entering for the router's home page. Refer to *Table 10-1: Configuration information for your router* for the value that is appropriate for your router.

b) Check the setting that determines how your browser connects to the Internet. Select **Start→Settings→Control Panel** and double-click on the **Internet Options** icon (for Windows XP, **Start→Control Panel→Network and Internet Connections→ Internet Options**). In the **Internet Properties** window, click the **Connections** tab. If you have entries in the **Dial-up settings** section, as shown in *Figure 17-2*, check **Never dial a connection**. This will allow you to start your web browser without directly connecting to your service provider's login service, since you will be using the router as the gateway.

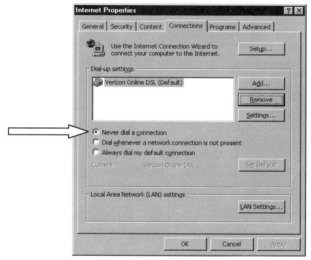

Figure 17-2: Internet Properties with Dial-up settings

If your settings look like *Figure 17-3*, you are already set up properly.

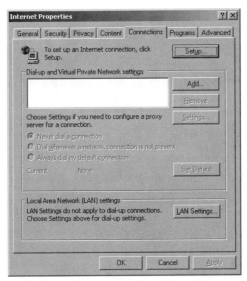

Figure 17-3: Internet Properties with no Dial-up settings

c) Check that that your browser is not set to "proxy" web requests. Proxies are web servers that service providers use to improve browsing performance by keeping frequently requested web pages readily accessible. Since your router has a private IP address, the proxy server will not be able to access the router's web page.

You will need to verify that your browser's proxy settings allow "local requests" to bypass the proxy server. See *Appendix G-4* for how to change the browser proxy settings.

35. I cannot access the router's home page or the Internet.

First, check your proxy settings as describe in *Item 34*. If that does not fix the problem, check to make sure your computer can "see" the router. Follow the steps in *Appendix G-1*.

If that test indicates a lack of network connectivity, verify the cabling between this computer and the router and any switches. Make sure that you have not erroneously used a "crossover" RJ-45 Ethernet cable. Also, make sure that you have not connected into a port labeled **WAN** on the router or switch. See *Section 17-11*,

Problems with configuring computers for additional help. Finally, check that the router and all switches are powered.

If you can "ping" the router but still cannot browse its home page, it is likely that your browser is not correctly configured. Follow the steps in *Item 34.*

17-12-1 Wired router

36. I have a network adapter installed in my computer. I have connected it to my router, but I cannot configure it.

First, check that you have applied power to the router.

Next, check the cabling to make sure that you have not connected the cable into the **uplink** jack of the router (if the router has a port labeled uplink). It will NOT work that way.

Next, check the configuration settings of the network adapter to make sure you have configured it to **Obtain an IP address automatically** and **Disable DNS** (see *Item 29*). If all this is correct, then reboot your machine and try again.

If you still cannot "see" the router with your browser, you may have your browser set up to **proxy** web requests. You will need to change this. See *Item 34.*

37. I have done all the above, and I still cannot see the router configuration page.

Check *Table 10-1* for the IP address of your router. It is possible that the manufacturer is using a different address. You should check your router's documentation.

It is possible that someone configured your router to respond to an IP address other than the value shown in the table or in the router's documentation. Most routers have a **reset** button to restore it to the factory settings. Look for the reset button on the front or back panel of the router. Make sure that the router has power and then press and hold the reset button for about 10 seconds. The indicator lights on the router should flash and sequence a bit.

If you have done this properly, the router should now respond to the IP address shown in *Table 10-1* or in the router's documentation. Use your browser to access the router again.

If it still does not work, it is likely that either your network adapter or your router is faulty. A more remote possibility is that the cable is faulty. Try replacing each in turn.

17-12-2 Wireless router

38. I cannot access my wireless router from my computer.

Try configuring the wireless router using a computer cabled directly to it. See answers to *Items 36* and *37* above.

17-13 Problems with switches

39. The computers that connect to a switch cannot access the Internet.

First, make sure that the switch has power. Next, make sure that the connection from your computer (or computers) to the switch is correct, and that none of them plugs into an **uplink** jack on the switch. If one does, you must move it to another jack.

Next, check the connection between the switch and the router. Check to make sure that both ends of the cable are not in **uplink** jacks and that you have not used a crossover cable.

17-14 Problems with network access

40. I can access and/or configure the router, but I cannot browse the Internet.

First, it is possible that the router and the cable or DSL modem are not "talking." Verify that you have connected them correctly with an RJ-45 Ethernet cable, that you connected this cable to the WAN port in the router, and that you have not used a "crossover" RJ-45 Ethernet cable. If you used a "crossover" cable, you must replace it. You should power off the router and then power on the router and restart your computer.

Next, check to see that the cable or DSL modem is powered. Remember, sometimes it takes a few minutes for it to "synchronize" with the network. If the modem is powered, use your browser to make sure you can access the router's home page.

If your network was functioning properly and you cannot reach sites on the Internet, it is likely that you are experiencing a network failure. If this persists longer than a few minutes, you may want to contact your service provider to inquire about network status.

If there are no reported network outages in your area, you need to see if you can send packets beyond your router onto the Internet. You can do this by checking Internet connectivity (see *Appendix G-2*). If you can reach sites on the Internet, the router and the access to your provider are almost certainly functioning correctly.

If the problem persists and you cannot browse the Internet, check *Item 41*.

If you still cannot reach sites on the Internet, it is likely that you are experiencing a network failure or some communications problem with your modem or access to your service provider. You may want to contact your provider's help desk for assistance.

41. My Internet connectivity checks out OK but I still cannot browse the Internet.

If your network was functioning properly and you have Internet connectivity (see *Appendix G-2*) but you cannot reach sites on the Internet, it is likely that you are experiencing a DNS failure on the service provider network.

You should try the Internet connectivity check (see *Appendix G-2*) by using a well-known website, such as www.irs.gov. If DNS does not resolve the IP name to an IP address, then there is most likely a network failure. You should call your service provider and find out the network status.

42. When I try to access the network, I get an error message about IP address conflicts.

For example, the error message in *Figure 17-4* is from a Windows 98 computer indicating that there is a conflict with another component of the network.

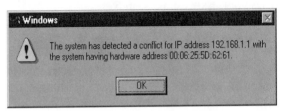

Figure 17-4: Error message - two computers with the same IP address

Check to see that your computer is set up to obtain its IP address dynamically. If you have assigned a fixed IP address to your computer, make sure that you have not assigned it an address that the router would also assign.

You may also need to check the other computers in your network, since one of them may have a static IP address. When you find it, change it as described in *Item 29*.

17-15 Problems with email

43. I cannot get my email to work on any of my computers.

Your broadband service provider usually provides your email service. You need to contact them and follow all their instructions in order to make it work. We give instructions on setting up email for one user. If you have multiple email accounts, repeat these steps using the appropriate email name and password for each user.

You need your email name and password set ahead of time by your service provider. They will normally set this up for you, and tell you what the name and password are.

During installation, you filled in the template in *Appendix A-2*. Included are values for your email name and password, and the IP addresses for your service provider's POP3 and SMTP servers. You will need this information to configure your email client. Your service provider should give detailed instructions on how to set up your email. If not, call their help desk.

Make sure you configure your email client to use the Local Area Network to connect to the mail servers (and not dialup connections!). In the paragraphs below, we illustrate the email settings for Microsoft Outlook Express version 5.

Begin by selecting **Start→Programs→Outlook Express** (or **Start→All Programs→Outlook Express** for Windows XP). You may get a window (*Figure 17-5*) asking you to choose whether Outlook Express should be your default mail client. This question will come up if you were previously using a different email client. In most instances, you should click **Yes**.

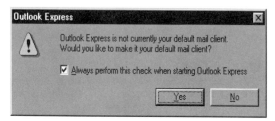

Figure 17-5: Initial Outlook Express dialog

On the menu bar, select **Tools→Accounts....**

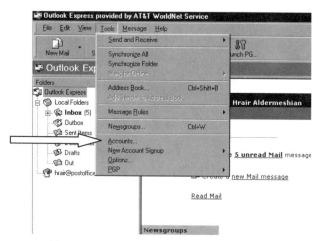

Figure 17-6: Start configuring email account

 A new window will appear that will allow you to set the email account settings. In this window, enter the name you would like to call your mail server, your name, and your full email name in both the **E-mail address** and **Reply address** fields.

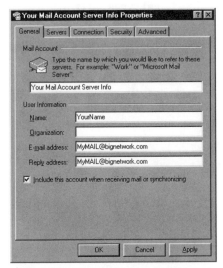

Figure 17-7: Set up account information

After filling in your personal information, select the **Servers** tab and fill in the POP3 and SMTP server information along with your email account name and password. If your service provider requires outgoing mail authentication, check that item off.

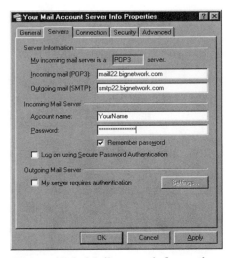

Figure 17-8: Mail server information

Click the **Connections** tab and specify in the drop-down menu that you always use the **Local Area Network** to connect to your email account.

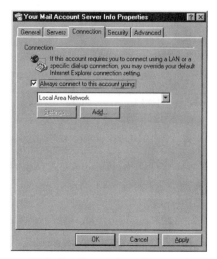

Figure 17-9: Set Local Area Network option

Next, click the **Advanced** tab and enter information about security related items (e.g., this account uses SSL). The example below shows SSL for both POP3 and SMTP.

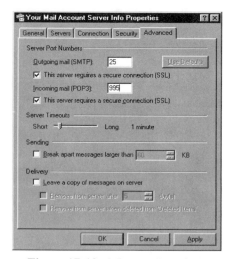

Figure 17-10: Advanced settings

Finally, click **OK**. You should be done. If mail still does not work, you will need to call your service provider for more help.

17-16 Problems with browsing

44. I cannot use the browser to access the router's home page, but I can access the Internet.

See *Item 34.*

45. I cannot access the router's home page or the Internet.

See *Item 35.*

46. I can access and/or configure the router, but I cannot browse the Internet.

See *Item 40.*

17-17 Problems with passwords

47. I cannot remember the password for the router.

The only thing you can do is to restore the router to its factory default settings. Most routers have a **reset** button that will restore it to the factory settings. You will have to make sure that the router has power and then press and hold the reset button (look for a small button on the front or back panel) for about 10 seconds. The indicator lights on the router should flash and sequence a bit, and after about thirty seconds, the router will have stabilized. You should have just reset the password to the factory default, see *Table 10-1.*

48. I cannot remember the password to my computer.

You may need to reinstall Windows. This process will allow you to create a new password while keeping your files. You may need to reinstall some applications, however.

The moral here is "don't forget your password." See *Section 16-4* for help.

17-18 Problems with viruses

49. When I turn on my computer, it is very sluggish or exhibits strange or unusual behavior when performing ordinary tasks such as word processing or email.

First, check to see if the virus-scanning software is performing a periodic check of your files now. If so, it will keep your disks busy and make applications run slower. Wait for it to finish.

Otherwise, run the virus-scanning software to verify that your computer is free of viruses. This is a good time to update the virus-scanner's virus definition files by visiting the website or the service provided by your virus-scanning software provider. Then run the virus-scanning software to see if you have any viruses in your computer.

You may want to verify that you have enabled **Auto-Protect** (Norton AntiVirus) or **Enable System Scan** (McAfee VirusScan). See the instructions in *Appendix J*, if you are using Norton AntiVirus, or in *Section 11-8*, if you are using McAfee VirusScan.

50. When the virus-scanning software detects a virus, I cannot clean it or delete it.

If your virus-scanning software is not capable of cleaning the virus, make a note of the virus name, numbers, and version. Then, visit the website of the virus-scanning software provider to see if they have specific instructions on how to eliminate the virus.

In most instances, if the virus, Trojan horse, or worm is in a file that is in a folder normally used for temporary files (e.g., `\Temp`, `\Windows\Temp`, `\Windows\Temporary Internet Files`) it is safe to delete it. In other instances, you may have to delete files from the Program Files or Windows system folders. Be careful in doing this in order to avoid making your computer unstable. Always keep a record of what you did to aid recovery if needed. If you are not comfortable deleting files from your Program Files or Windows system folders, you will need to seek professional help.

51. When I opened an email attachment, my email client software started behaving strangely. I can see many email messages in my Outbox.

A virus undetected by your virus-scanning software may be the cause. First, you should disconnect this computer from your network to prevent it from further spreading the virus. If your computer uses a wired connection, you should disconnect it by removing the blue RJ-45 Ethernet cable or the USB cable. If your computer uses a PC Card (PCMCIA) or USB network adapter, you should remove the card or device. If your computer connects using a wireless device, you will need to disable the network adapter. See *Appendix B-5*.

Now that you have isolated this computer, it is time to shut down all applications and see how to clean the virus by running the virus-scanning software. Usually, it will be able to identify the virus. If not, visit the website of your virus-scanning software provider for updated virus definition files or further steps to take to clean the virus.

Once you have successfully cleaned the virus, reverse your steps and reconnect and/or reset the network adapter.

17-19 Problems with file/printer/device sharing

17-19-1 Network access problems

52. When I open the My Network Places or Network Neighborhood folder to see the computers on my mini-internet, I am denied access to the network.

First, check and make sure that your computer is part of your workgroup. See *Section 17-11-3*.

Second, if you see a window similar to *Figure 17-11*, you need to set permissions on the file or print server to allow network access. Enabling "guest" permissions is the easiest way to do this. (You can also add a user account to the file or print server for each user in the network that needs access. This is a bit more cumbersome, but a bit more secure.) We show how to do this for servers running Windows

2000. You need "administrator" privileges to complete the following steps (see *Item 26*).

Figure 17-11: Network authentication window

In Windows XP, select **Start→Settings→Control Panel→User Accounts**. In other versions of Windows, select **Start→Settings→Control Panel** and double-click on **Users and Passwords** to display the list of authorized users (*Figure 17-12*).

In Windows XP, if the **Guest account is off**, click on the **Guest** icon and click the **Turn On the Guest Account** button. In other versions of Windows, to check if the "guest" account is properly enabled, select the **Advanced** tab and click on the **Advanced** button in the **Advanced User Management** section to display the **Local Users and Groups** window. Select **Users** on the left side of the window (*Figure 17-13*). This should expand the list of authorized users on this file or print server.

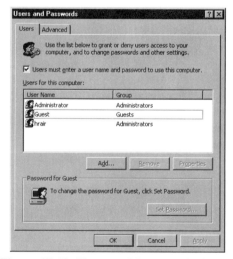

Figure 17-12: Users and Password window

Figure 17-13: Local users and groups

Right-click on the "guest" account and select **Properties** from the menu to display its properties. Clear the **Account is disabled** check box and click **OK**. Close the **Local Users and Groups** window by clicking the close button (⊠) in the upper right corner. Click **OK** to close the **Users and Passwords** window.

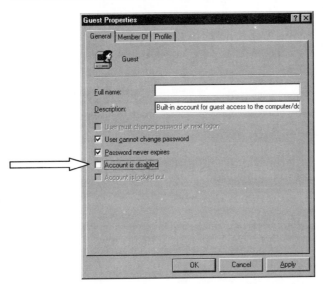

Figure 17-14: Guest account properties

From the client computer, try again to access the shared folder or printer. If you no longer receive the "network authentication" request (*Figure 17-11*), you have fixed the problem.

Third, if you get a message similar to the error message shown in *Figure 17-15* indicating Windows does not recognize your computer as part of your mini-internet, try rebooting.

Figure 17-15: Windows network error message

If that does not work, reset the IP settings for your network adapter. See *Appendix B-5*.

Try browsing the mini-internet again by opening the **My Network Places** or **Network Neighborhood** folder.

17-19-2 File sharing

53. When I try to read or write files in other computers on the mini-internet, I am blocked.

See *Item 52*.

17-19-3 Printer sharing

54. I have tried to use the Add Printer Wizard to install a network printer, and it did not work.

If your computer is running Windows XP or Windows 2000, you should first check to make sure that you have **administrator** privileges. If not, you should log in as administrator and try running the wizard again.

Next, check to see that you can access the network printer. In Windows XP, you select **Start→Control Panel→My Network Places** and click **View workgroup computers** under **Network Tasks**. In other versions of Windows, you can test this by opening the **My Network Places** or **Network Neighborhood** folder and clicking **Computers Near Me** or **Entire Network** and click on the workgroup. Then select and click on the name of the computer that is the print server for the printer you are trying to install. If the printer is visible on your screen that means your computer has access to that network printer.

You need to have the proper software in your computer to print. If the Windows system of your computer is different from the Windows system on the printer's print server, you may need to install the specific drivers for that printer in your computer. First, follow the instructions given by the printer's manufacturer for sharing the printer on a network. If that does not work, the steps that follow usually correct the problem.

Find the software CD that came with the printer. Note: If you cannot find the software CD, visit the web page of the printer manufacturer to download the software.

 The instructions below are for a printer connected to a print server named **HRAIRNT** and a shared printer that we have named **hpdeskjet**. Make sure you replace these with your names!

On the client computer, insert the CD in your CDROM and follow the manufacturer's directions on installing the software. If the printer software specifies that the printer be attached to the LPT1 port, click OK and continue with the installation.

When asked to test the printer, click **skip** because your printer is not really connected to your computer's LPT1 port.

Complete the software installation of the printer software by following the rest of the install steps.

For Windows XP or Windows 2000:

In Windows XP select **Start→Control Panel→Printers and Other Hardware→Printers and Faxes**, in Windows 2000 select **Start→Settings→Printers**. Right-click the **hpdeskjet** icon, select **Properties** and select the Ports tab. Click **Add Port...**

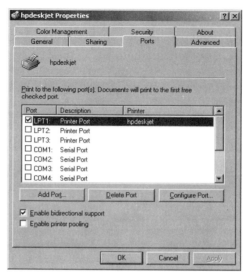

Figure 17-16: Printer port details for Windows 2000/XP

Make sure you select **Local Port** (Yes! That is right: Local Port!) and click **New Port**. Where indicated, enter the full network name of the network printer, in this case \\HRAIRNT\hpdeskjet. Click **OK**.

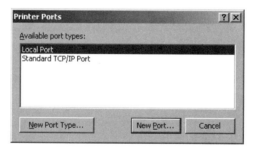

Figure 17-17: Windows 2000/XP port dialog window

Figure 17-18: Entering network printer name, Windows 2000/XP

You have specified the path for accessing the printer. Click **OK** to complete the installation of your network printer.

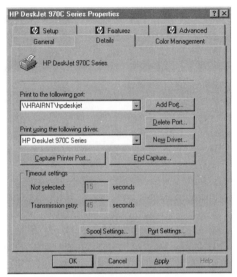

Figure 17-19: Printer properties - added network printer to port

For Windows 98 or Windows ME:

Select
Start→Settings→Printers→hpdeskjet→Properties and select
the **Details** tab.

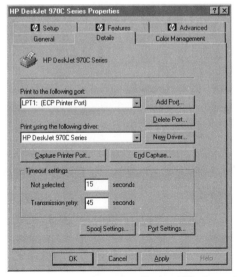

Figure 17-20: Printer port details for Windows 98/ME

Click **Add Port**. A new window will appear. Make sure that you select the **Network** option, and enter the full network name of the printer in the field (in this case, `\\HRAIRNT\hpdeskjet`). Click **OK** in this and the **Properties** window to complete the settings.

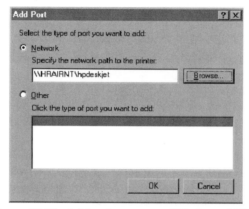

Figure 17-21: Add printer port - Windows 98/ME

55. Whenever I try to print a document on a shared printer, nothing happens.

First, check to see that the particular printer that you are using is listed in your **Printers** folder. Select **Start→Setting→Printers** (in Windows XP select **Start→Control Panel→Printers and Other Hardware→Printers and Faxes**). The **Printers** window lists all the printers that are accessible from this computer. In this example, we need to access a printer named `hpdeskjet` connected to a print server called `HRAIRNT`.

Make sure that the printer icon is displayed in the **Printers** window. If it is not there, use the **Add Printer** icon. Remember it is a network printer and should be specified as such. See *Section 12-2*.

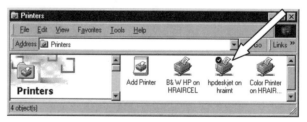

Figure 17-22: Printers folder

Otherwise, right-click on the specific printer icon that you are attempting to use. The menu shows various settings for the specific printer. Make sure the **Pause Printing** or **Use Printer Offline** settings are not checked. If they are, click to remove the check marks.

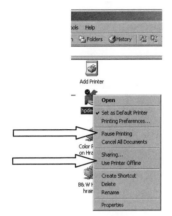

Figure 17-23: Make sure Pause Printing and Use Printer Offline are not checked

56. **When I try to print a document on a shared printer, I get an error message.**

First, check to see that the printer is listed in the **Printers** folder. Select **Start→Settings→Printers** (in Windows XP select **Start→Control Panel→Printers and Other Hardware→Printers and Faxes**). If the printer is not listed, use the **Add Print Wizard** to add that printer to your list. See *Section 12-2*.

Is the shared printer powered? Is its print server powered and running?

Figure 17-24: Cannot print on shared printer

Figure 17-25: Another error with a shared printer

Next, check to see if the error message indicates a network access problem. The windows in *Figure 17-24* and *Figure 17-25* indicate that Windows is not able to access the printer's print server. See *Section 17-19-1* to see if you can solve this problem and then retry printing.

Appendixes

Templates

This appendix includes a number of templates that help you collect the important network settings, plan network layout and implement your mini-internet. Some of the information you need comes from your broadband service provider. You also need to create a list of your computers, peripherals, and their locations. Main sections of this book cover the details of how to collect and go about using the information.

In addition to these templates, you probably will want to keep a record of billing, help desk, technical support, and other relevant information that your service provider may provide to you.

A-1 Questions for your network installer

If you have decided to hire someone to install your network, you will find it useful to have a list of questions to ask to make sure the installation proceeds appropriately. The checklist below lists a set of general questions that provide a good start. You will likely need to amend these to fit your particular situation. The questions pertain to the set up of home and office networks and do not cover cost, timing, schedule, and other related business decisions.

A-1-1   Installation checklist

o   Which broadband service provider you recommend?

>   o   Cable or DSL?

>   o   Why?

o   Does your installation include a cable/DSL router?

o   Are you arranging for my broadband service, or will I need to contact the provider?

- o   When do I need to contact the Cable or DSL provider to arrange for service?

- o   Are you going to install the Cable or DSL modem or will the service provider install it?

o   Are you going to create an inventory of computers, printers and other devices that will connect to the network?

- o   When do I need to review it?

o   Do you recommend a wired or wireless network?

- o   Why?

o   If you are going to use wired network components, what kind of wiring will you use?

- o   Cat-5E?

- o   Cat-5?

o   Where do you recommend we place the cable or DSL modem and the router?

- o   Will we have easy access to test the cable or DSL modem and the router?

o   Are you going to configure the wired or wireless router?

o   Do you recommend a firewall?

- o   What do you recommend for maintenance and support?

o   If you are going to use wireless network components, will you set the 128-bit WEP keys on the wireless portion of the network?

o   Are you going to install all the network adapters in the computers and laptops?

- o   Are you going to configure the wired network adapters?

- o   Are you going to configure the wireless network adapters?

o   Are you going to install the printers and enable printer sharing?

o   Are you going to configure the print server and the other computers that access the printers?

o   Are you going to enable folder and file sharing?

o   Are you going to configure the file server and the other computers that access the folders and files?

o   Will the network and printers be fully functional when you are done with the installation?

o   Will you install virus-scanning software in the computers?

o   Will you make sure that my computers receive virus definition file updates?

A-2 Information from service provider

Question to ask your provider		If yes, you need this information
If you are using DSL, does your provider use PPPoE?	Yes ☐ No ☐	User name: _____ (e.g., ver87coast) DSL Password: _____
Does your provider require a specific hostname and domain name?	Yes ☐ No ☐	Hostname: _____ (e.g., sjbac128) Domain name: _____ (e.g., cableco.net)
Has your provider given you a static IP address?	Yes ☐ No ☐	IP address: ___.___.___.___ (e.g., 10.117.44.153) Subnet Mask: ___.___.___.___ (e.g., 255.255.255.0) Gateway: ___.___.___.___ (e.g., 10.117.44.1) DNS server1: ___.___.___.___ (e.g., 10.117.44.4) DNS server2: ___.___.___.___ (e.g., 10.221.1.4)
Does your provider support email?	Yes ☐ No ☐	Full email name: _____ (e.g., newuser@cableco.net) POP3 server: _____ (e.g., mail.cableco.net) SMTP server: _____ (e.g., smtp.cableco.net) Outgoing mail authentication? Yes ☐ No ☐ SSL for POP3? Yes ☐ No ☐ (if Yes, SSL port number: ____, e.g., 995) SSL for SMTP? Yes ☐ No ☐ (if Yes, SSL port number: ____, e.g., 465)

A-3 Information about your computers

Description of Computer	Name of Computer	Description of Printer	Location

A-4 List of needed components

Item	Quantity	Length	Description

A-5 Information you need to set up your network

Information	Value
Service provider phone number	
Service provider help desk phone number	
IP address of router	
Router username	
Router password	
SSID (if wireless router)	
WEP phrase (if wireless router)	
WEP key (if wireless router)	
Channel number (if wireless router)	
Modem manufacturer	
Modem serial number	
Workgroup name (for file and printer sharing)	

B

Installing Network Adapters

B-1 Installing a PCI network adapter

To install a PCI network adapter into your computer, you need to be comfortable "opening up" your computer, inserting the network adapter in an available PCI slot, and "closing up" your computer. If you are not comfortable doing this, we suggest that you bring your computer and the network adapter to a local shop equipped to do this for you.

If you are prepared to do this yourself, here is a roadmap of the steps you need to follow:

1. Power off your computer. Remove the power cord, and remove all cables currently connected to the computer, carefully label and mark the cables and the sockets so that you will be able to reconnect them easily.

2. Following the directions provided in your computer's user manual, remove the computer's cover. Make sure you have the appropriate tools, usually a small Phillips or "Torx" screwdriver.

3. Locate an available PCI slot. If there are no available PCI slots, buy and use a USB network adapter if your computer supports USB. See *Appendix B-3*.

4. Remove any cover protecting the rear of the PCI slot, but retain any small screw. Insert the network adapter, making sure you properly seat it in the slot, by exerting uniform pressure all along the top of the network adapter. Make sure you do not disturb any wiring or cabling inside your PC. Insert and tighten the retained small screw to hold the network adapter in place.

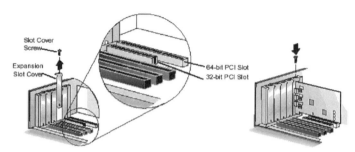

Figure B-1: PCI slots (Used with permission of Adaptec, Inc.)

5. Replace the computer's cover; secure any screws or fasteners as described in the computer's user manual.

6. Restore all cabling. Finally, insert the power cord.

You are now ready to power on the computer and install any needed software drivers. Continue with steps outlined in *Appendix B-4*.

B-2 Installing a PC Card network adapter

Installing a PC Card (PCMCIA) network adapter is very simple. Just insert the network adapter into an externally accessible PC Card (PCMCIA) slot on your computer.

You are now ready to power on the computer, and install any needed software drivers. Continue with steps outlined in *Appendix B-4*.

If your computer does not have an available PC Card (PCMCIA) slot, buy and install a USB network adapter. Follow the steps in the next section.

B-3 Installing a USB network adapter

Installing a USB network adapter is usually very simple. Just follow the manufacturer's instructions that come with the device.

Most of the time you can just insert the connector into an available USB port in your computer or USB hub.

Figure B-2: USB hub

You are now ready to power on the computer, and install any needed software drivers. Continue with steps outlined in *Appendix B-4*.

If your computer does support USB but does not have an available USB port, obtain a USB hub, move one existing USB connection from the computer to the hub, and insert the hub's connector in the USB port you just made available. You can now install the USB network adapter in an available port on the hub. Continue with the steps outlined in the next section.

 If you cannot find a PCMCIA or USB port to connect a network adapter or you are running Windows 98 First Edition, your best route is to take the computer to a retailer, who can determine if they can install an internal adapter.

B-4 Installing drivers and other software

Restart your computer and log on. When your computer boots up, Windows should automatically detect the newly inserted network adapter, and start the process of installing needed software drivers. If your system fails to detect the new adapter, see *Chapter 17, Consolidated Troubleshooting* for next steps.

In general, follow the steps outlined in the documentation that came with your adapter. However, to provide a guide, we detail the process of installing drivers for a particular network adapter (3Com USB 10/100 Ethernet Adapter) on a computer running Windows 2000. The process is similar in most other cases, except for Windows XP: it usually recognizes and installs the appropriate driver without any intervention.

It is possible that Windows already has a copy of the needed software. If so, it will notify you and may request you to restart the computer. In most cases, however, you need to monitor the software installation process and point out the location where the software can be found (usually, on the CD that came with the adapter).

 In the following paragraphs, we show the software installation steps for a 3Com USB 10/100 Ethernet Adapter. Remember that your installation could be slightly different.

When the computer starts, Windows should detect the new device and display the window similar to *Figure B-3*.

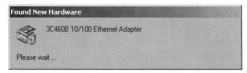

Figure B-3: Computer recognized USB network adapter

If Windows already has a usable device driver installed, the process will complete and you can use the network adapter. Otherwise, Windows will start the **New Hardware Wizard** to locate and install the appropriate software.

Figure B-4: New Hardware Wizard starting window

Click the **Next** button. The wizard will identify the new device (in this case, a 3Com USB 10/100 Ethernet Adapter). It is usually safest to select the recommended **Search for a suitable driver for my device**.

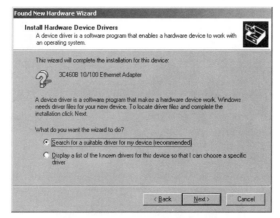

Figure B-5: Guiding the wizard

After you click the **Next** button, the wizard will show you a list of locations that it can search for a suitable driver. If your network adapter came with a CD or floppy, load it now, and select the appropriate check box in the **Locate Driver Files** window.

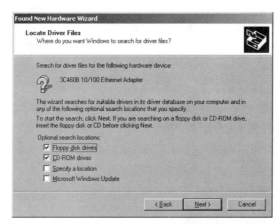

Figure B-6: Indicating where to find the driver

When you click the **Next** button, the wizard will search each selected location (e.g., Floppy disk drive, CD-ROM drive, etc.) for the suitable driver.

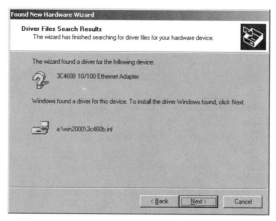

Figure B-7: Wizard found driver, installing

The wizard should find the correct driver and report it in the **Driver Files Search Results** window. If the wizard cannot find a valid driver, it reports it here. You should verify that you have inserted the correct CD or floppy. Next, you may need to point the wizard at the folder that contains the valid driver. You should follow the manufacturer's directions. As a last resort, you may need to obtain new drivers from the manufacturer. You can do this either by contacting the manufacturer or by visiting the manufacturer's website. For additional help, see *Chapter 17, Consolidated Troubleshooting* for next steps.

If the wizard finds a valid driver, it asks you to approve the installation of the driver. You do this by clicking the **Next** button.

Figure B-8: Wizard completes installation

Congratulations! Click the **Finish** button and you are done! Depending on the device and on your version of Windows, you may need to reboot. If prompted to do so, reboot, and continue with installing your network.

B-5 Resetting the network adapter settings

In unusual cases, you may need to reset the IP address and other network settings of your network adapter. You instruct your operating system to release the IP address and other settings assigned to your network adapter and then reassign new ones. This action sometimes fixes problems of accessing your network or shared printers and folders.

You can also use this technique to isolate your computer when you think that a virus may have infected your computer. In that case, enable network adapter to reassign a new IP address only after you believe that you have cleaned the virus from your computer.

For Windows XP:
Select **Start→Control Panel→Network and Internet Connections→Network Connections**. Right-click on the icon for your network adapter, and select **Disable**. Wait about 30 seconds. Right-click again on the icon for your network adapter, and select **Enable**.

For Windows 2000:
Select **Start→Settings→Network and Dialup Connections**. Right-click on the icon for your network adapter, and select **Disable**. Wait about 30 seconds. Right-click again on the icon for your network adapter, and select **Enable**.

For Windows ME and Windows 98:
Select **Start→Run**. In the window that appears, enter `winipcfg` and hit enter.

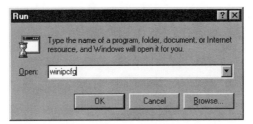

Figure B-9: Run winipcfg

An **IP Configuration** window should appear displaying the network adapter address and the private IP address assigned to your computer. If not, select it from the drop-down list.

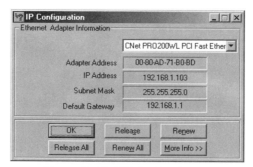

Figure B-10: Winipcfg window

Click the **Release All** button. This will release the IP address and network settings assignment.

Then, click the **Renew All** button. This will reassign the private IP address and network settings to your network adapter.

C

Configuring Windows XP

C-1 Configuring the network

Windows XP has wizards that do most of the work to set up your network adapter and your network. The easiest way to get your computer set up is to get the wizard running.

You need to configure the network adapter settings. The simplest way of doing this is to make a new network connection in the **Network Connections** window. Select **Start→Control Panel→Network and Internet Connections→Network Connections**. That should bring up the **Network Connections** window.

Figure C-1: Network Connections window

Click **Create a new connection** in the upper left hand corner to bring up the **New Connection Wizard**. Click **Next**.

Figure C-2: New Connection Wizard

Select **Connect to the Internet**. Click **Next**.

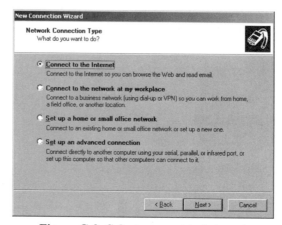

Figure C-3: Select connect to internet

Select **Set up my connection manually**. Click **Next**.

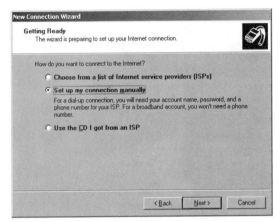

Figure C-4: Selecting setup type

Select **Connect using a broadband connection that is always on**. Click **Next**. If you are using a DSL modem, for the "first" Windows XP computer very likely you will be asked to select **Connect using a broadband connection that requires a user name and password**. In addition, you may have to register your account with the DSL service provider. Please follow the instructions that they gave you.

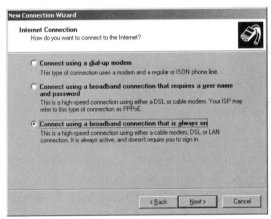

Figure C-5: Your connection will always be on!

Windows XP should have properly configured your network adapter settings. Click **Finish** and you are done.

Figure C-6: Finishing the new connection wizard

Next, configure the mini-internet settings by assigning a name to your computer and identifying your workgroup name. The simplest way of doing this is to run the Windows XP **Network Setup Wizard**.

Each computer must have a unique name in order to distinguish it from all others within the mini-internet. If your computer does not have a name or workgroup name assigned, this is the time to specify them. For this purpose, we recommend using the computer names you listed on your inventory sheet (see *Section 6-1*). It is easiest to use the name HOME or OFFICE for the workgroup entry. See *Section 12-1* for further details on workgroups.

You start this wizard from **My Network Places** folder. Select **Start→My Computer**. Click the **My Network Places** link under **Other Places** to open the **My Network Places** folder.

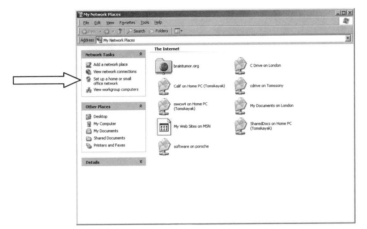

Figure C-7: My Network Places folder

Select **Setup a home or small office network** in the upper left hand corner of the window under **Network Tasks**. This should start the **Network Setup Wizard**.

Figure C-8: Starting the Network Setup Wizard

Click **Next** in this and the following informational window.

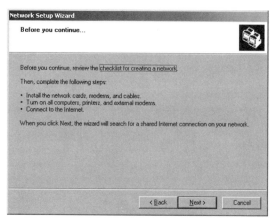

Figure C-9: Click Next!

Windows now asks how this computer connects to the Internet. Since you are using a router (Microsoft calls this a residential gateway), make sure to select **The computer connects to the Internet through another computer on my network or a residential gateway**.

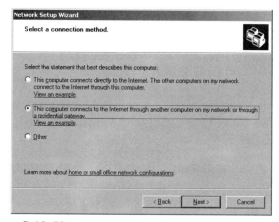

Figure C-10: You connect to the Internet through a router

You can now give your computer a name and some text that describes this computer. This information will be visible to the other computers on your mini-internet. Click **Next** after entering the description and name.

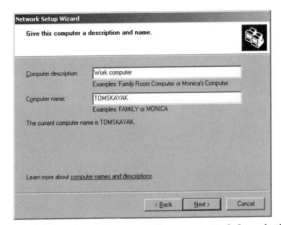

Figure C-11: Give the computer a name and description

Enter the name you have chosen for your network's workgroup. To make sure that Windows can identify and share all the resources in your mini-internet, you must enter the same workgroup name in each computer in your mini-internet. Click **Next**.

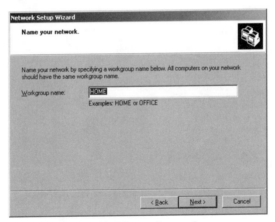

Figure C-12: Name the workgroup

Windows XP summarizes the network settings and its progress in *Figure C-13*. Click **Next**.

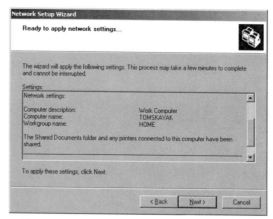

Figure C-13: Summary of network settings

Select **Just finish the wizard; I don't need to run the wizard on other computers**, click **Next**.

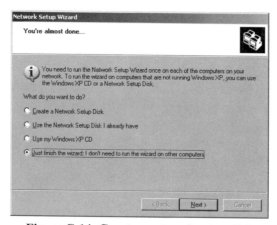

Figure C-14: Create a network setup disk

Finally, click **Finish**.

Figure C-15: Completed running network setup wizard!

That is it! Your network adapter and your network settings should now be configured properly.

C-2 Configuring a wireless network adapter

Windows XP has built-in support for wireless network adapters and networks. In general, there is no need for special client software for each wireless network adapter. We show the hardware installation and configuration of the wireless network adapter.

Insertion of the device causes Windows XP to start the **New Hardware Wizard**.

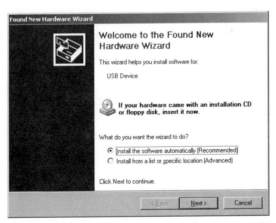

Figure C-16: Windows XP starts the hardware wizard

Insert the CD provided with the device in the CD drive, and then click **Next**.

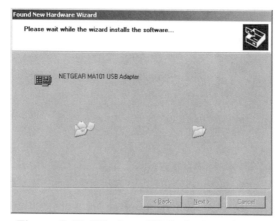

Figure C-17: Windows XP finds the software

The installation process is quite automatic. Windows finds the appropriate software on the CD and installs it. That is all there is to it. Hardware and driver installation is complete. Click **Finish**.

Figure C-18: Windows XP completes installing software

As soon as the installation completes, Windows detects the presence of wireless network components, and prompts you to configure the adapter. Click the balloon on the right bottom corner of your screen. This displays the wireless configuration window.

Figure C-19: Windows XP detects wireless network components

Notice that Windows displays the network name (SSID) you set in your wireless router. There may be more listed, if there are other wireless networks nearby. Make sure you choose your wireless network name in the list. Using the record of the **WEP** key you made in the template in *Appendix A-5*, carefully copy the 26 character **WEP** key into the field labeled **Network key** and click **Connect**.

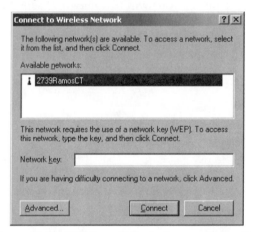

Figure C-20: Windows XP wireless configuration

Windows has completed configuring the adapter. Within a few seconds, it should report that the wireless connection is set up.

Figure C-21: Windows XP connects to your wireless network

If not, you should see *Chapter 17, Consolidated Troubleshooting* for next steps.

You can review or modify any of the wireless settings by displaying the **Wireless Network Connection Properties** window shown in *Figure C-22*. You display this window by selecting **Start→Control Panel→Network and Internet Connections→Network Connections**. Right-click on the icon for your wireless network, select **Properties** and click on the **Wireless Networks** tab.

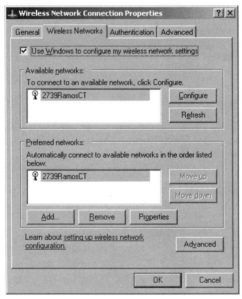

Figure C-22: Windows XP - Wireless connection properties

Finally, test the wireless network adapter configuration by following the steps in *Section 10-6-4*.

D

Configuring Windows 2000

D-1 Configuring the network

If you are using Windows 2000, you have to set up your network adapter and your mini-internet.

You need to configure the network adapter settings.

Select **Start→Settings→Network and Dial-up Connections**.

Double-click the **Local Area Connection** icon to open it.

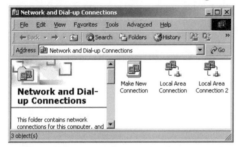

Figure D-1: Network connections setup window

In the **Local Area Connection Status** window, click **Properties**.

Figure D-2: Selecting Properties in Local Area Connection Status

259

Select the **Internet Protocol (TCP/IP)** line. Then click **Properties**.

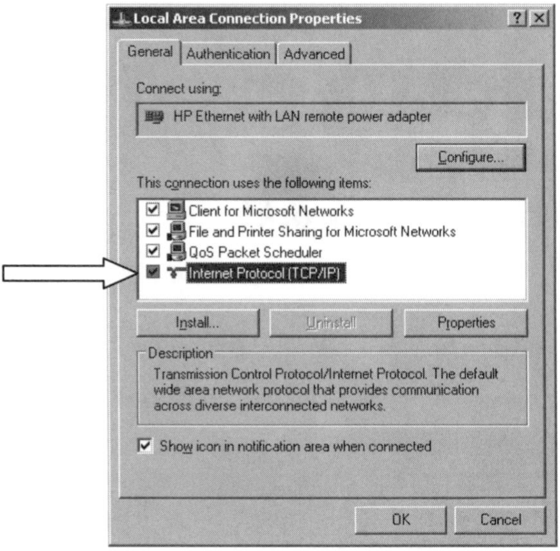

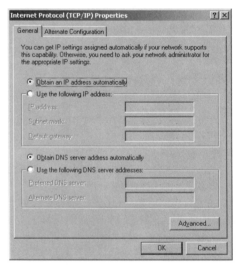

Figure D-3: Configure Internet Protocol (TCP/IP)

Select both **Obtain and IP address automatically** and **Obtain DNS server address automatically**. Click **OK** to return to the **Local Area Connection Properties** menu. Click **OK** again.

Figure D-4: TCP/IP Properties

You are done with the setup of the network adapter!

Next, configure the mini-internet settings by assigning a name to your computer and identifying the workgroup name.

Each computer must have a unique name in order to distinguish it from all others within the mini-internet. If your computer does not have a name or workgroup name assigned, this is the time to specify them. For this purpose, we recommend using the computer names you listed on your inventory sheet. It is easiest to use the name HOME or OFFICE for the workgroup entry. See *Section 12-1* for further details on workgroups.

Select **Start→Settings→Control Panel**. This will open the **Control Panel** window. Double-click on the **System** icon to display the **Systems Properties** window.

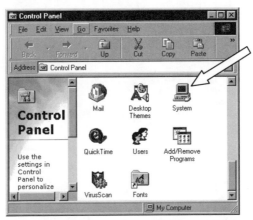

Figure D-5: Control Panel - double-click on System icon

There should be a tab labeled **Network Identification**. Select it. You should see a window similar to the one in *Figure D-6*.

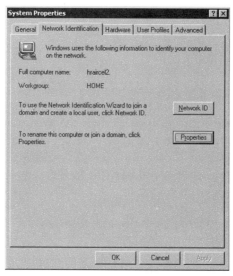

Figure D-6: System properties

Click **Properties** to open the **Identification Changes** window.

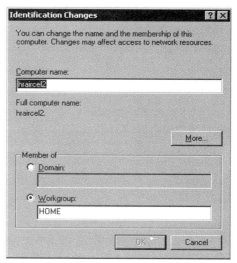

Figure D-7: Change computer and workgroup names

Select the **Workgroup** option and enter the name of the workgroup in the entry field. In this example, we use HOME as the workgroup name. If appropriate, set the name of the computer in the indicated field.

Click **OK** on this and the previous windows in order to make the changes permanent for this computer. That is it! Your network adapter and your network settings should now be configured properly.

D-2 Configuring a wireless network adapter

We detail in the following paragraphs the process of configuring a particular network adapter (NETGEAR USB wireless network adapter model MA101) on a computer running Windows 2000. The process will be similar for Windows ME and Windows 98. Windows XP has built-in support for wireless network adapters. We show in *Appendix C-2* how to configure wireless network adapters in Windows XP.

The configuration process requires you to install specialized software provided by the wireless network adapter manufacturer, and to use this software to set identical value for SSID and WEP settings as your router. Use the template in *Appendix A-5* where you collected the SSID and WEP values of your router. Finally, test the configuration to make sure you can access your network.

D-2-1   Installing the wireless client software

You need to install the appropriate client software on each computer that has a wireless network adapter.

Insert the CD provided with your wireless adapter in the CD drive. If the software setup starts automatically, follow the steps outline on the screen. Sometimes, you need to start the "Client Software Installation" process, by double-clicking on the **Setup** icon in the Windows Explorer window.

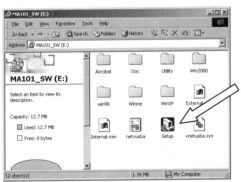

Figure D-8: Contents of CD - double-click on Setup

This should get the installation process started. If not, verify that the correct CD is in the CD drive. You should see a window showing the software about to be installed (Figure D-9). If the window does not identify the correct software or hardware, exit the installation by clicking **Cancel**. Find and insert the proper CD. Otherwise, proceed by clicking **Next**.

 Remember, we are using the NETGEAR MA101 USB adapter for this example. The particular network adapter you have installed may show slightly different windows.

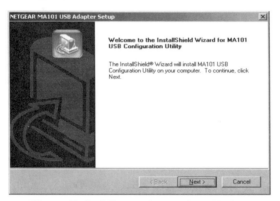

Figure D-9: Client software installation

As is usual with a software installation, the installer gives you every opportunity to change default locations. You can safely accept the defaults and click **Next** on this and the following window.

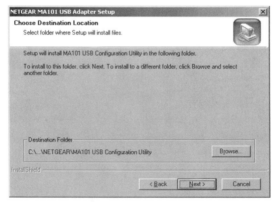

Figure D-10: Choose the default destination for the software

After you click **Next**, the installer starts work in earnest copying files and making the appropriate settings in your computer. The entire process should only take a minute or two.

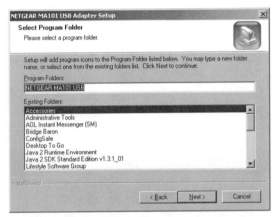

Figure D-11: Select the default Program Folder

Wait until the installation is complete. Click **Finish**.

Figure D-12: Installation complete!

Depending on the adapter and your version of Windows, it may ask you to reboot your computer. If asked, do so.

D-2-2   Configuring the wireless client software

First, start the client software. The installer usually configures things so that the client software will start automatically each time you boot the computer. The first time, however, you may need to start it manually. It is easiest to do this through the **Start** menu. In this example, select **Start→Programs→NETGEAR MA101 USB→Configuration Utility** to start the program.

 Remember, we are using the NETGEAR MA101 USB adapter for this example. The particular network adapter you have installed may have slightly different windows.

Notice the added icon in the System Tray on the right bottom corner of your screen. Double-click on it to pop up the client adapter utility window.

Figure D-13: Client icon in system tray

This should start the client utility. A window similar to that shown in *Figure D-14* should appear. If not already visible, select the **Status** tab by clicking it.

Figure D-14: NETGEAR MA101 USB client utility

You use the fields in the **Status** window to set the **SSID** (your wireless network group name) of the network adapter. Without this information, your wireless network adapter will not connect to your router. Use the template in *Appendix A-5* where you collected the SSID and WEP values of your router. Click on the **Status** tab to display it. Clicking on the **Change** button will highlight several of the fields, as shown in *Figure D-15*.

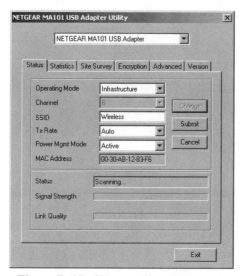

Figure D-15: Client utility- Status tab

You may leave the other fields at the default settings, but you must enter your wireless network's name in the field labeled **SSID** and click **Submit**. This causes the client utility to configure the wireless network adapter with this value. If done correctly, within several seconds, you should notice the **Status** field change to **Associated**, and the **Signal Strength** and **Link Quality** meters become active.

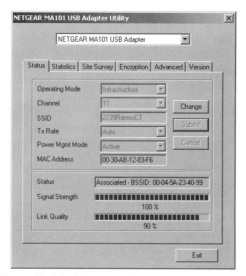

Figure D-16: Client utility - after setting SSID

This means your wireless network adapter and your wireless router have noticed each other. However, without the identical **WEP** settings (encryption and security keys), you will not be able to send IP packets between them. Select the **Encryption** tab by clicking it.

You should see the window shown in *Figure D-17*. You need to set two fields here: first, select **128 Bit** from the drop-down menu for the **Encryption** field, and second, set the **WEP** key. Within the **Encryption** field, pick the **128 Bit** mode for **Encryption**. This allows you to enter the **WEP** key.

Next, using the record of the **WEP** key you made in the template in *Appendix A-5*, carefully copy the 26 character **WEP** key into the field labeled **Key #1**. See *Figure D-18*. You may leave the other fields set at their default values. These values are set in the adapter when you click **Submit**.

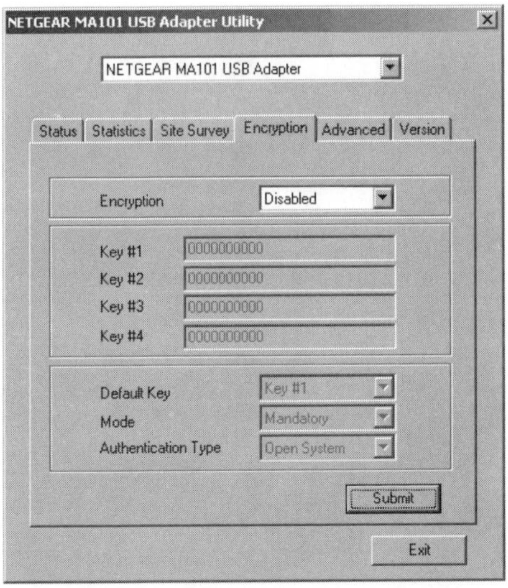

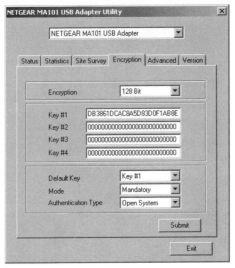

Figure D-17: Client utility - prior to setting WEP values

Figure D-18: Client utility - WEP key set

That should be it: your wireless network adapter and your wireless router should now communicate. To verify this, you can select the **Statistics** tab. You should see numbers on the **Successful** lines. If you see increasing number of **Unsuccessful** packets, it probably means you did not type the **WEP** key correctly. Try again.

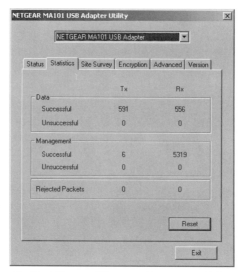

Figure D-19: Client utility - notice successful packets!

Finally, test the wireless network adapter configuration by following the steps listed in *Section 10-6-4*.

E

Configuring Windows ME

E-1 Configuring the network

If you are using Windows ME, you must configure the settings for your network adapter manually and then use the Home Networking wizard that does most of the work to set up your mini-internet

You need to configure the network adapter settings. Select **Start→Settings→Control Panel**. This will open the **Control Panel** window (*Figure E-1*). Double-click the **Network** icon to display the **Network** window (*Figure E-2*).

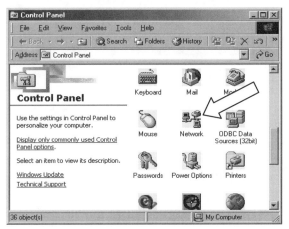

Figure E-1: Control Panel - double-click Network icon

There should be a tab labeled **Configuration**. Select it. You should see a window similar to the one in *Figure E-2*. Select from the list of installed network components the line that begins with "**TCP/IP→**" and contains the name of your network adapter. Click **Properties**.

271

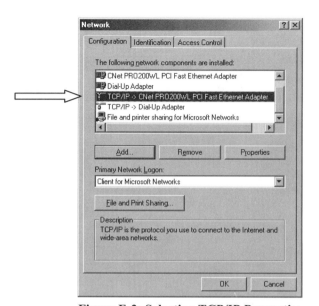

Figure E-2: Selecting TCP/IP Properties

Select **Obtain an IP address automatically** in the **IP Address** tab.

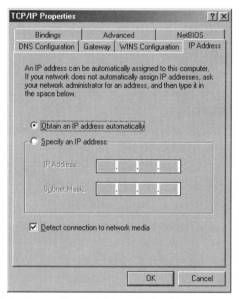

Figure E-3: Activating Obtain an IP address automatically

Select **Disable DNS** in the **DNS Configuration** tab. Click **OK** to return to the **Network** settings menu.

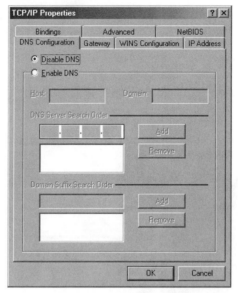

Figure E-4: Disabling DNS

Click **OK** again in the **Network** window *Figure E-2*. You are done with the setup of the network adapter!

Next, configure the mini-internet settings by assigning a name to your computer and identifying your workgroup name. The simplest way of doing this is to run the Windows ME **Home Networking Wizard**.

Each computer must have a unique name in order to distinguish it from all others within the mini-internet. If your computer does not have a name or workgroup name assigned, this is the time to specify them. For this purpose, we recommend using the computer names you listed on your inventory sheet. It is easiest to use the name HOME or OFFICE for the workgroup entry. See *Section 12-1* for further details on workgroups.

You start this wizard from **My Network Places** folder.

Figure E-5: My Network Places folder

There should be an icon labeled **Home Networking Wizard**. Double-click it.

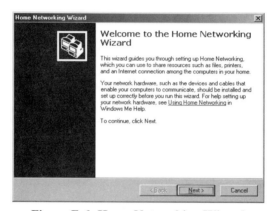

Figure E-6: Home Networking Wizard

This will open up the wizard. Click **Next**.

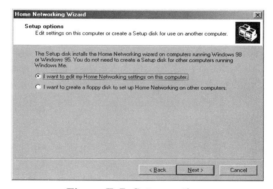

Figure E-7: Setup options

Select **I want to edit my Home Networking settings on this computer**.
Click **Next**.

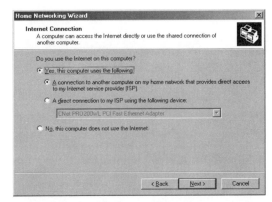

Figure E-8: Internet Connection options

Select **A connection to another computer on my home network that provides direct access to my Internet service provider (ISP)**. Click **Next**.

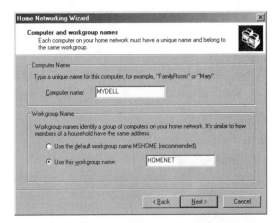

Figure E-9: Setting computer and workgroup names

Enter a unique computer name and the workgroup name for your mini-internet. In this example, we use MYDELL for the computer name and HOMENET for the workgroup name. Click **Next**.

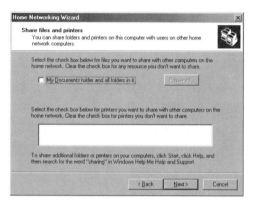

Figure E-10: File and printer sharing options

Do not check anything on the next screen. Click **Next**.

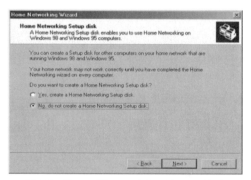

Figure E-11: Home Networking Setup disk option

Check, **No, do not create a Home Networking Setup disk**. Click **Next**.

Figure E-12: Completing the Home Networking Wizard

Next, click **Finish**. You are done!

E-2 Configuring a wireless network adapter

We detail in *Appendix D-2* the process of configuring needed settings for a particular network adapter (NETGEAR USB wireless network adapter model MA101) on a computer running Windows 2000. The process is similar for a computer running Windows ME.

The configuration process requires you to install specialized software provided by the wireless network adapter manufacturer and to use this software to set identical values for SSID and WEP settings as your router. Finally, test the configuration to make sure you can access your network.

You only need to install this software on each computer that has a wireless network adapter. If you have previously installed the client software, you can safely skip the installation steps and get right to running the client software as outlined in *Appendix D-2-2*.

Finally, test the wireless network adapter configuration by following the steps listed in *Section 10-6-4*.

F

Configuring Windows 98

F-1 Configuring the network

If you are using Windows 98, you must configure the settings for your network adapter and mini-internet manually.

You need to configure the network adapter settings.

Select **Start→Settings→Control Panel**, and double-click **Network**.

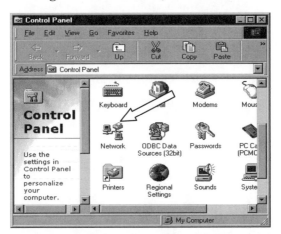

Figure F-1: Control Panel - double-click Network icon

There should be a tab labeled **Configuration**. Select it. Then, select from the list of installed network components the line that begins with "**TCP/IP→**" and contains the name of your network adapter. Click **Properties**.

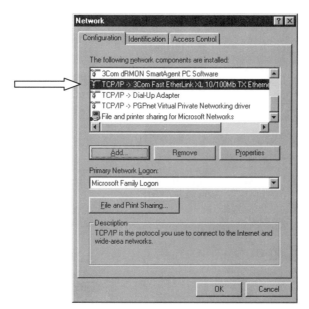

Figure F-2: Selecting TCP/IP Properties

Select **Obtain and IP address automatically** in the **IP Address** tab

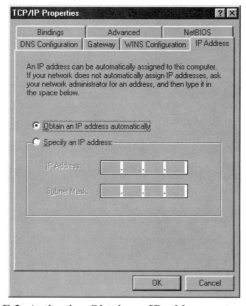

Figure F-3: Activating Obtain an IP address automatically

Select **Disable DNS** in the **DNS Configuration** tab. Click **OK** to return to the **Network** settings menu.

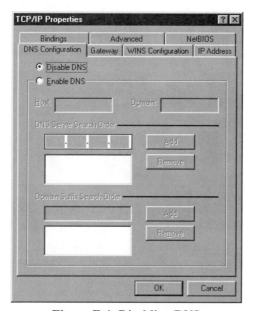

Figure F-4: Disabling DNS

Click **OK** again in the **Network** window *Figure F-2*. You are done with the setup of the network adapter!

Next, configure the mini-internet settings by assigning a name to your computer and identifying your workgroup name.

Each computer must also have a unique name in order to distinguish it from all others within the mini-internet. If your computer does not have a name or a workgroup name assigned, this is the time to specify them. For this purpose, we recommend using the computer names you listed on your inventory sheet. It is easiest to use the name HOME or OFFICE for the workgroup entry. See *Section 12-1* for further details on workgroups.

Click the **Identification** tab in the **Network** window *Figure F-2*.

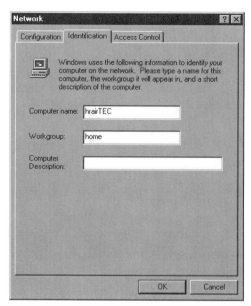

Figure F-5: Change computer and workgroup names

Enter your workgroup name in the **Workgroup** field. In this example, we use home as the workgroup name. If appropriate, set the name of the computer in the indicated field (in this example, our computer is named hrairTEC).

Click **OK** in this and the previous window to make the changes permanent. That is it! Your network adapter and your network settings should now be configured properly.

Your computer may tell you that it needs to reboot. If so, reboot now. You are done!

F-2 Configuring a wireless network adapter

We detail in *Appendix D-2* the process of configuring needed settings for a particular network adapter (NETGEAR USB wireless network adapter model MA101) on a computer running Windows 2000. The process is similar for a computer running Windows 98.

The configuration process requires you to install specialized software provided by the wireless network adapter manufacturer and to use this software to set identical values for SSID and WEP settings as your router. Finally, test the configuration to make sure you can access your network.

You only need to install this software on each computer that has a wireless network adapter. If you have previously installed the client software, you can safely skip the installation steps and get right to running the client software as outlined in *Appendix D-2-2*.

Finally, test the wireless network adapter configuration following the steps listed in *Section 10-6-4*.

G

Configuring Internet Options

G-1 Quick check of connectivity

First, check to make sure your computer can "see" the router. To do this, you ask the computer to "ping" the router. That is, you ask the computer to send a special IP packet directed to the router. When the router receives this packet, it immediately replies with an acknowledgement of its receipt. This way, you know that the computer's settings are correct, that the cabling is correct, and that the router is powered and working.

 Note that in the following example, we use the private IP address assigned to Linksys routers (192.168.1.1). If you are using another router, replace this address with the proper one. See *Table 10-1*.

To ask the computer to send this packet, you must activate a **Command Window**. You do this as follows:

For Windows XP:
Select **Start→All Programs→Accessories→Command Prompt**.

Windows 2000:
Select **Start→Programs→Accessories→Command Prompt**.

For Windows ME:
Select **Start→Programs→Accessories→MS-DOS Prompt**.

For Windows 98:
Select **Start→Programs→MS-DOS Prompt**.

A window similar to *Figure G-1* should appear. Carefully type **ping 192.168.1.1** (using the IP address appropriate for your router) and press the enter key. (You are asking your computer to execute the **ping** command, which sends a series of IP packets to the address given, in this case **192.168.1.1**, the default IP address of the Linksys router.)

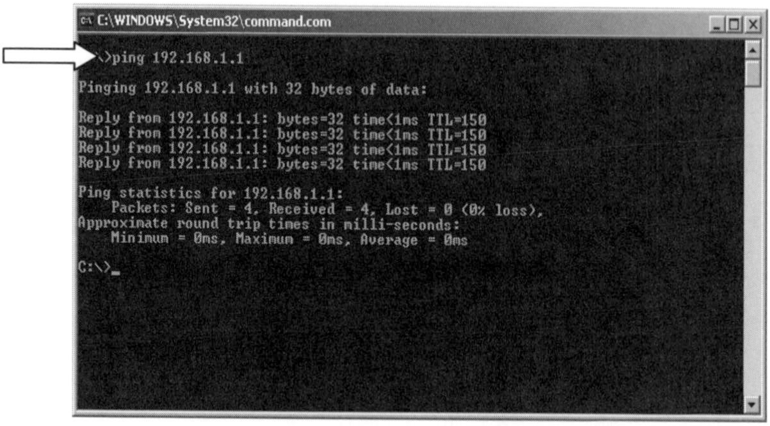

Figure G-1: Results of "pinging" router

If you see a report similar to the above, showing "**Reply from 192.168.1.1 ...**," you have set up everything correctly to this point. Congratulations! If you see a report of "**Request timed out**" or no response at all, something is amiss that you need to correct before proceeding. You should see *Chapter 17, Consolidated Troubleshooting* for next steps.

G-2 Checking Internet connectivity

You can check whether packets from your computer are reaching the Internet by asking your computer to "tracert" a known IP name or IP address. That is, you ask the computer to send a special IP packet to every network element on the Internet on the path to this IP name or IP address. When these network elements receive this packet, they immediately reply with an acknowledgement of its receipt. This way, you know that the computer's settings are correct, that the cabling is correct, that the router is powered and working, and that the connection to your service provider is up and running.

To ask the computer to send this packet, you must activate a **Command Window**. You do this as follows:

For Windows XP:
Select **Start→All Programs→Accessories→Command Prompt**.

Windows 2000:
Select **Start→Programs→Accessories→Command Prompt**.

For Windows ME:
Select **Start→Programs→Accessories→MS-DOS Prompt**.

For Windows 98:
Select **Start→Programs→MS-DOS Prompt**.

 Note that this test requires the use of an Internet address of a well-known site. In the example, we use the IP name `www.irs.gov` and the IP address `66.77.65.247`. You can replace this with the IP address of any other well-known site. The IP addresses reported in the **tracert** window will then be different.

A window similar to *Figure G-1* should appear. Carefully type **tracert www.irs.gov** and press the enter key. (You are asking your computer to execute the **tracert** command, which starts the process of checking every Internet network element on route to the destination site.

If you see a report similar to Figure G-2 showing "**Tracing route to www.irs.gov [66.77.65.247] ...**", check to see that there are IP addresses, such as 10.108.120.1, listed in the window. It is OK if you see some "**Request timed out**" entries in the list. If you see IP addresses listed, you have set up everything correctly and your Internet connection is function correctly. Congratulations!

If **tracert** responds differently, for example, if it reports "**Unable to resolve target system name...**", you can run one more check to ascertain whether the DNS server of the service provider is functioning properly. Carefully type **tracert 66.77.65.247** and press the enter key. If you get a report that lists IP addresses, such as 10.108.120.1, then you have network connectivity but non-functioning DNS. If the report lists no IP addresses, your connection to the service provider is not working. In either case, you should call your service provider and find out the network status.

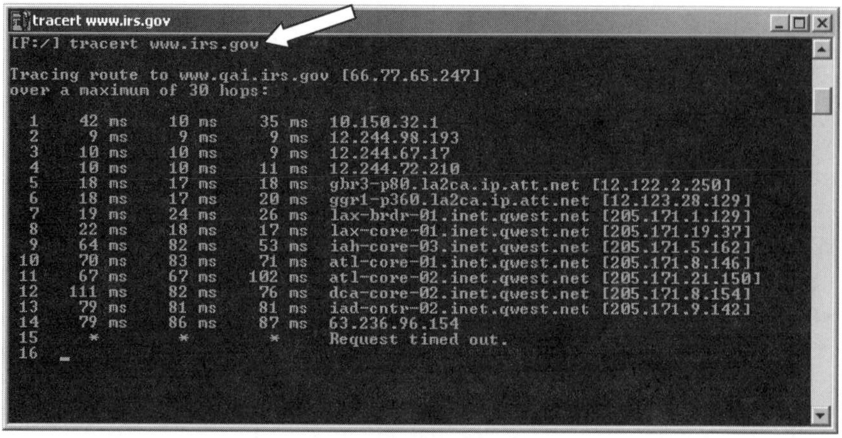

```
tracert www.irs.gov                                                    _ □ ×
[F:/] tracert www.irs.gov

Tracing route to www.qai.irs.gov [66.77.65.247]
over a maximum of 30 hops:

  1     42 ms     10 ms     35 ms  10.150.32.1
  2      9 ms      9 ms      9 ms  12.244.98.193
  3     10 ms     10 ms      9 ms  12.244.67.17
  4     10 ms     10 ms     11 ms  12.244.72.210
  5     18 ms     17 ms     18 ms  gbr3-p80.la2ca.ip.att.net [12.122.2.250]
  6     18 ms     17 ms     20 ms  ggr1-p360.la2ca.ip.att.net [12.123.28.129]
  7     19 ms     24 ms     26 ms  lax-brdr-01.inet.qwest.net [205.171.1.129]
  8     22 ms     18 ms     17 ms  lax-core-01.inet.qwest.net [205.171.19.37]
  9     64 ms     82 ms     53 ms  iah-core-03.inet.qwest.net [205.171.5.162]
 10     70 ms     83 ms     71 ms  atl-core-01.inet.qwest.net [205.171.8.146]
 11     67 ms     67 ms    102 ms  atl-core-02.inet.qwest.net [205.171.21.150]
 12    111 ms     82 ms     76 ms  dca-core-02.inet.qwest.net [205.171.8.154]
 13     79 ms     81 ms     81 ms  iad-cntr-02.inet.qwest.net [205.171.9.142]
 14     79 ms     86 ms     87 ms  63.236.96.154
 15      *          *          *   Request timed out.
 16
```

Figure G-2: Result of "tracert"

G-3 Changing network settings

In case you need to update your computer's network settings, we give here only high-level steps needed to complete the process. To keep the overall process simple and clear, we have included the details for different versions of Windows in separate appendices. Please refer to *Table G-1* for the sections appropriate to your version of Windows.

Power on the computer and log in. If your computer is running Windows XP or Windows 2000, you need to make sure that you have **administrator** privileges. If you do not have administrator privileges, ask someone who does to implement these steps for you. (If no one can log in as administrator, you may need to reinstall Windows).

Version of Windows	Where to read next!
XP	*Appendix C*
2000	*Appendix D*
ME	*Appendix E*
98	*Appendix F*

Table G-1: Where to find your network configuration material

Repeat these steps on each of your remaining computers, if necessary.

G-4 Changing the browser settings

To surf the Internet using a browser, it is critical that your computer's operating system and your browser have the proper Internet settings. During the installation and registration of your "first" computer, your service provider may change these settings to fit their specific network characteristics. It is essential to change these settings to work with your network.

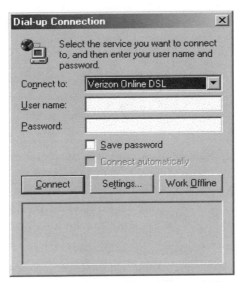

Figure G-3: Dial-up Connections window

For example, you may have problems using your browser if your computer was previously set up to use a dial up connection to the Internet. In addition, if you used an installation CD from your DSL provider, the **Internet Options** may be set in a way that causes a dial up connection window (*Figure G-3*) to pop up every time you start your web browser. Editing the **Internet Options** parameters fixes these problems.

Select **Start→Settings→Control Panel→Internet Options** (in Windows XP select **Start→Control Panel→Network and Internet Connections→Internet Options**) to access the **Internet Properties** window as shown in *Figure G-4*. Click the **Connections** tab.

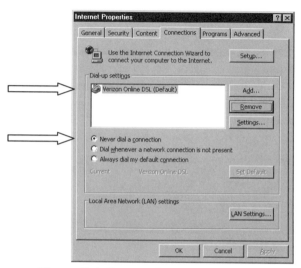

Figure G-4: Internet Properties with Dial-up setting

If you have entries in the **Dial-up and Virtual Network settings** section, select **Never dial a connection** if it is not already selected. This instructs your computer to start your web browser without first connecting to the DSL service. Remember, your router directly connects to your DSL service. It logs in for you. If your settings look like *Figure G-5*, you are already set up properly.

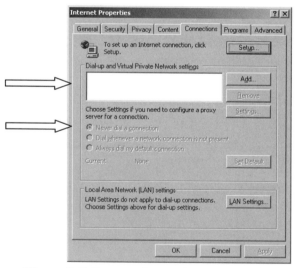

Figure G-5: Internet Properties with no Dial-up settings

Next, verify that your browser is set up correctly to access the router's home page. Some ISPs require the use of a "proxy server" for browsing the web. If your ISP requires it, you need to make an additional setting so that your browser can access your router's home page. Click the **LAN Settings** button in *Figure G-5*. You should see a window similar to the one in *Figure G-6*. If the box labeled **Use a proxy server for your LAN** is not checked, your ISP does not require a proxy and you are done. Close this window by clicking **OK**.

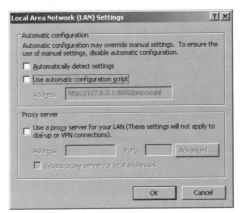

Figure G-6: If "Use a proxy ..." is not checked, you are OK!

If **Use a proxy server for your LAN** is checked, make sure **Bypass proxy for local addresses** is also checked. See *Figure G-7*. Click **OK** to make these changes final.

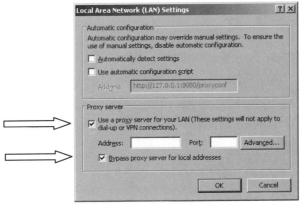

Figure G-7: If "Use a proxy ..." is checked, check "Bypass proxy ..."

You make all these changes permanent by clicking on **OK** in the **Internet Properties** window in *Figure G-8*.

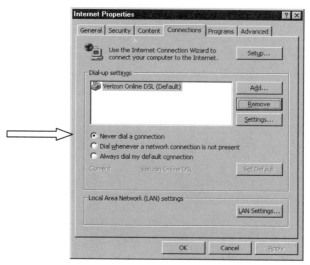

Figure G-8: Internet Properties with Never dial a connection

Configuring NETGEAR Router

H-1 Configuring NETGEAR routers

Now that you have your network set up, and you have the "first" computer properly configured, the next step is to configure the router. This allows the router to identify itself to your service provider's network, and allows it to begin routing IP packets between your computers and the Internet. In this arrangement, the router appears as a computer connected to the cable or DSL provider's network.

Start your browser to access the router's configuration page. The router you have installed conveniently responds as if it were a web server. This makes configuring it as simple as starting your Web browser (i.e., Microsoft Internet Explorer or Netscape Navigator) and asking it to retrieve the page addressed by the router's IP address.

 In the following examples, we are showing the windows and details from a NETGEAR router. The particular router you are configuring may display slightly different windows. **We strongly recommend that you perform these steps with a computer wired to the router, not one with a wireless connection to it.**

Enter the IP address of the router's home page (for the NETGEAR router you enter `192.168.0.1`) into the address panel of your browser and hit the enter key.

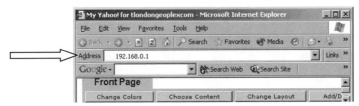

Figure H-1: Requesting the router's home page

293

You should see the pop up window shown in *Figure H-2*, asking you to enter a **User name** and a **Password**. This is the normal security check built into the router to prevent unauthorized access to the router's settings. (If you see this window pop up again, very likely you took a long time to modify the router settings, re-enter the **User Name** and **Password** to continue.)

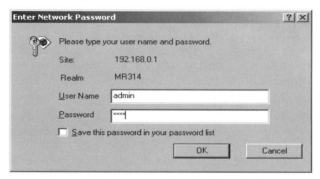

Figure H-2: Router authentication window

If your browser does not bring this pop up window but displays a dialup connection or an error message, you need to take remedial action before you can proceed. Please read *Appendix G, Configuring Internet Options*. After you fix the settings of your internet properties and browser settings, continue with configuration of your router. Enter the IP address of your router and see if you get the pop up window shown in *Figure H-2*.

The NETGEAR router is factory set with a password of **1234**. Enter `admin` in the **User Name** field, enter `1234` as the **Password** field, and click **OK**. (Don't worry about the password at this point. We show you how to change this later.) You should see the router's home page displayed. (*Figure H-3* shows the home page of a wireless NETGEAR router.) For most networks, you need to check or set a few settings. However, if you are using a wireless router, it is essential that you enter the proper security settings in order to avoid unrestricted wireless access to your mini-internet.

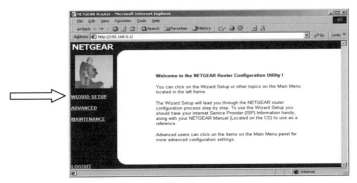

Figure H-3: Router's home page

At this point, you configure the router's network settings. This task should be either easy or straightforward, depending on the type of configuration settings your cable or DSL provider expects. In the simplest case, the router needs almost no configuration. Otherwise, it requires a few lines of careful typing.

H-2 Using the setup wizard

From the router's home page (*Figure H-3*), click on the **WIZARD SETUP** hyperlink. The wizard will display a series of pages into which you enter the information you collected in the template in *Appendix A-2*. Enter the **Domain Name** if provided to you by your ISP. In the unlikely event that your service provider indicates that you need to set a **Host Name**, enter it in the **System Name** field now. Click **Next**.

Figure H-4: NETGEAR setup wizard

You will see the following page (*Figure H-5*) if you are configuring a wireless router. Otherwise, continue with the following section that best matches your service type.

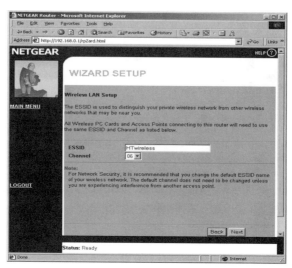

Figure H-5: Wireless network setup

Enter your wireless network name in the **ESSID** field (ESSID and SSID are both acronyms for your wireless network name). The **ESSID** applies only to the wireless components of your network and is different from the **Workgroup** name we described in *Section 3-2*. Enter a short and easy to remember name for your network. You may select the first eight to ten characters of your address, your last name, or anything. It should be easy for you to remember, but ideally hard for someone else to guess. Do not select easy to guess names, such as **Home**, **Office**, **MyNetwork**, or similar names that we suggested for **Workgroup** names. You do not need to change the Channel entry. Click **Next**.

If your service is DSL and your provider uses PPPoE, continue reading *Appendix H-2-1*. If your provider uses dynamic settings (DHCP), continue reading *Appendix H-2-2*. If your provider requires "static settings," read *Appendix H-2-3*. Finally, complete the wireless configuration by reading *Appendix H-3*.

H-2-1   Your service provider uses DSL and PPPoE

In the **ISP parameters for Internet Access** page, select the **PPP over Ethernet** option from the **Encapsulation** drop-down menu (PPPoE is a protocol that allows the service provider to authenticate users of the DSL service). Next, enter your DSL **User Name** and **Password** in the indicated fields. (Your DSL service provider gives these to you. You have recorded them in the template). You are enabling the router to take over the user name and password validation for your network. Set the **Idle Timeout** to 9999 seconds, to ensure that the IP connection is up most of the time unless the router is inactive for an extended period. Click **Next** in the bottom right corner of the **WIZARD SETUP** page.

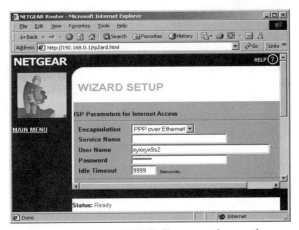

Figure H-6: WAN PPPoE connection option

Since your service automatically sets the IP address and other needed network settings, you need to make sure that the router has the **Get automatically from ISP** options selected for both **WAN IP address** and **DNS Server Addresses**. If these options are not set, select them now. Click the **Next** button on the bottom right corner of the page

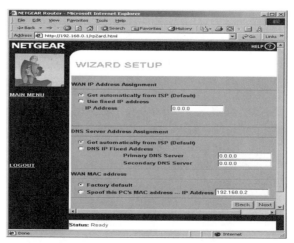

Figure H-7: Select Get automatically from ISP

Click **Finish** in the next page that appears and then click **LOGOUT**. If you are using a wireless router, jump to *Appendix H-3*. Finally, you should change the default password for the router. This is important to do. Otherwise, anyone with knowledge of it will be able to reconfigure your router. See *Appendix H-4* below.

H-2-2   Your service provider uses "dynamic" settings

In the **ISP parameters for Internet Access** page, select `Ethernet` from the **Encapsulation** drop-down menu. Do not change the **Service Type** field. See *Figure H-8*.

Your service automatically sets the IP address and other needed network settings as shown in *Figure H-7*. You need to make sure that the router has the **Get automatically from ISP** options selected for both **WAN IP address** and **DNS Server Addresses**. If these options are not set, select them now. Click the **Next** button on the bottom right corner of the page.

Figure H-8: Select Ethernet in Encapsulation drop-down menu

Click **Finish** in the next page that appears and then click **LOGOUT**. If you are using a wireless router, jump to *Appendix H-3*. Finally, the last step is to change the default password for the router. This is important to do. Otherwise, anyone with knowledge of the default router password will be able to reconfigure it. See *Appendix H-4* below.

H-2-3   Your service provider uses "static" settings

If your cable or DSL service provider assigns static IP addresses, you have a few more steps to complete the router's configuration. You already have all the needed information at hand, since you collected it from the service provider or installer to fill in the template in *Appendix A-2* (see *Table H-1*).

The static IP address provided by the operator has the following form xxx.xxx.xxx.xxx (e.g. `66.77.65.231`), that is, four numbers separated by periods. It is important to include all the periods and specify exactly the IP address specified by the cable or DSL provider. This IP address is your Wide Area Network (WAN) IP address, and each computer on the Internet uses it to talk to your computers.

Question to ask your provider		If yes, you need this information
If you are using DSL, does your provider use PPPoE?	Yes ☐ No ☐	User name: _____ DSL Password: _____
Does your provider require a specific hostname and domain name?	Yes ☐ No ☐	Hostname: _____ Domain name: _____
Has your provider given you a static IP address?	Yes ☐ No ☐	IP address: ____.____.____.____ Subnet Mask: ____.____.____.____ Gateway: ____.____.____.____ DNS server1: ____.____.____.____ DNS server2: ____.____.____.____
Does your provider support email?	Yes ☐ No ☐	Full email name: _____ POP3 server: _____ SMTP server: _____ Outgoing mail authentication? Yes ☐ No ☐ SSL for POP3? Yes ☐ No ☐ (if Yes, SSL port number: ____, e.g., 995) SSL for SMTP? Yes ☐ No ☐ (if Yes, SSL port number: ____, e.g., 465)

Table H-1: Information you need from your service provider

In addition to the static IP address, the service provider gives you your **domain name**, (e.g., verizon.com or home.attbi.com), and three other IP address-like settings. The first is your **subnet mask**. This is information that allows the various Internet routers to direct packets to and from you. It will probably be something like 255.255.255.0. Second is your **default gateway**. This is the IP address where your router should send all packets destined for the Internet (it is the "next router in the path"). Last are one or more IP addresses of the **DNS** you should use to translate IP names and URLs to IP addresses (see *Section 3-1-5*).

Make sure that you have correct values for these five parameters. If you do not have them, or you are not sure that the values you have are accurate, call your cable or DSL service provider. They can give you the information, usually over the telephone.

In the **ISP parameters for Internet Access** page (*Figure H-8*), select `Ethernet` from the **Encapsulation** drop-down menu. Do not change the **Service Type** field.

In the **WAN IP Address Assignment** page, select the **Use fixed IP address** option and enter your static IP address in the **IP Address** field, Subnet Mask in the **IP Subnet Mask** field, and Gateway in the **Gateway IP Address** field. Select the **DNS IP Fixed Address** and enter the values for DNS server1 and DNS server2 in the **Primary DNS Server** and Secondary DNS Server fields. Click **Next**.

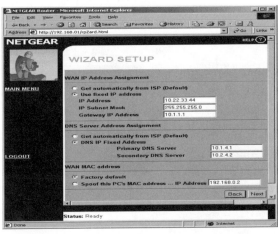

Figure H-9: Setting static IP address values

Click **Finish** in the next page that appears and then click **LOGOUT**. If you are using a wireless router, continue with *Appendix H-3*. Finally, the last step is to change the default password for the router. This is important to do. Otherwise, anyone with knowledge of the default router password will be able to reconfigure it. See *Appendix H-4* below.

H-3 Wireless router configuration

There are a few more steps to set up a wireless router. You need to make sure that the **wireless network name** (called the **ESSID)** and **encryption**

settings (called **WEP settings**) are set identically in your wireless network adapters and in your router.

 In the following examples, we are showing the windows and details from a NETGEAR router. Use appropriate entries to match your particular router.

To start, you configure these values in the router. As above, connect to the router with your browser by specifying the router IP address as the destination address, i.e. `192.168.0.1`. Again, **we strongly recommend that you perform these steps with a computer wired to the router, not one with a wireless connection to it.**

Click on the **ADVANCED** hyperlink on the left side. When a list of additional links appears below **ADVANCED**, click on the **WIRELESS** link to display the **WIRELESS LAN SETUP** page. Select the **Setup** tab at the top, if necessary.

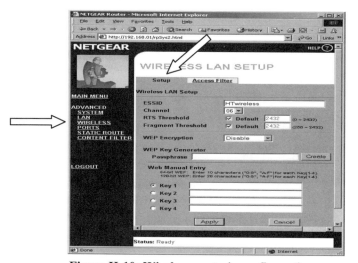

Figure H-10: Wireless router's configuration page

Notice the entry for **ESSID** (the wireless network name you previously entered in the WIZARD SETUP). The **Channel** field sets the particular radio channel used for wireless communications. You only need to change this if the signal strength is too weak or you get interference from other signal sources.

You need to enable **WEP Encryption** ("Wired Equivalent Privacy") so your network will not be open to anyone nearby with a wireless network adapter. Otherwise, strangers will be able to see all your traffic and insert new traffic without your knowledge. **You must change these values to establish the security of your wireless network.** You already changed the wireless network name, ESSID. Now you need to enable **WEP Encryption**. In its drop-down menu, select `128-bit WEP`.

Next, select another easy to remember but very hard to guess key phrase (e.g., the last few words of your favorite song or poem). Enter it in the **Passphrase** field and click the **Create** button. You should see a sequence of twenty-six numbers and letters appear in the **Key 1** field.

You should print this page or write down the values you selected for **ESSID**, **Channel**, and **WEP Key**. Use the template in *Appendix A-5*. You will need this information later to configure the wireless network adapters.

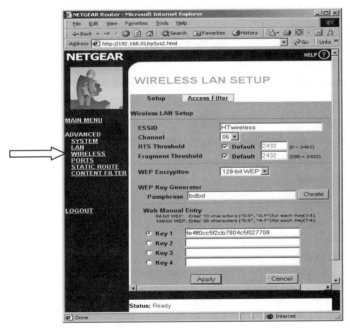

Figure H-11: Setting your encryption key

If you have wireless network adapters from the same manufacturer as the router, all you need to do is remember the pass phrase. Otherwise, and more likely, you must enter the actual twenty-six characters of the key into each wireless network adapter manually. Very carefully, write the letters and numbers that comprise the key on a piece of paper. Double check to make sure you copied it correctly. Use the template in *Appendix A-5*.

Make sure to click **Apply** at the bottom of the **WIRELESS LAN SETUP** page and click **LOGOUT**. In *Section 10-6-1*, you will use the software that manages the wireless network adapter to set its **wireless network name** and **wireless encryption settings** to these identical values. If the settings on the router and the wireless network adapters do not agree, they will not "talk," and your computers will not be part of your network.

H-4 Set the password on the router

Connect to the router with your browser by specifying the router IP address as the destination address, i.e. `192.168.0.1`.

Enter `admin` for the **User name**, enter the current router password (the default one is `1234`) in the pop up window. Click **OK**.

Click on the **ADVANCED** hyperlink on the left side of the router's home page. When a list of additional links appears below **ADVANCED**, click on the **SYSTEM** link. Select the **Password** tab in the top and center of the page. You set the router's password through this page.

In the appropriate fields, enter the old and new passwords (twice to make sure you have typed it correctly!). Remember this password or pass phrase. You will need to enter it each time you want to access the router's configuration pages. Click the **Apply** button.

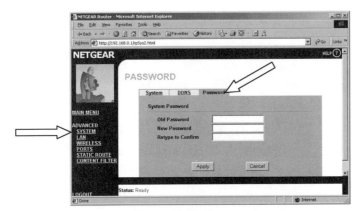

Figure H-12: Password page

That is it! Remember to change it again at the appropriate interval.

Wireless Only Installation

I

We strongly recommend that you set up and configure your wireless router using a computer directly wired to it. This provides a degree of safety and simplicity, since you can easily recover if you accidentally mis-configure the wireless router or wireless network adapter. Accidentally mis-configuring them while attempting a completely wireless installation can leave you unable to connect to the router using your wireless network adapters. Therefore, your best approach is to use an RJ-45 Ethernet cable to connect a computer to the router and follow the instruction for a wired installation (see *Section 10-2*).

If you must do a completely wireless installation, you need to follow these steps carefully.

1. Power on the router. Make sure the cable or DSL modem is powered off.

2. Start a computer that is close to your wireless router, preferably in the same room. You should have already installed the wireless network adapter and its client software. If not, see 10-6-1.

3. The default state of the wireless router allows wireless communication, but each vendor uses a different default SSID (wireless network name, called ESSID on some routers and network adapters). You need to set the network adapter on this computer to use the appropriate SSID that is right for your router. You can find your router's SSID in *Table I-1* or in the router's manual.

4. Set the SSID in your network adapter to the default value for your router using the client software installed with your wireless network adapter. When properly set, this computer should be able to communicate with the router.

Router Type	IP address	User Name	Initial Password	SSID if wireless
Linksys	192.168.1.1	(None, leave blank)	admin	linksys
NETGEAR	192.168.0.1	admin	1234	Wireless
DLink	192.168.0.1	admin	(None)	default
SMC (wired)	192.168.2.1	(None)	(None)	default
SMC (wireless)	192.168.123.254	(None)	admin	default

Table I-1: Configuration information for your router

5. Use your browser (e.g., Internet Explorer) and the appropriate IP address from *Table I-1* to access the router's home page. When prompted, use the appropriate User Name and Password. You should follow the sequence described in *Section 10-2* or *Appendix H-1*.

6. You need to modify the process described in *Section 10-2-4* or *Appendix H-3* for changing the SSID and the WEP encryption settings. You must make these changes in two steps, first change the SSID in the router and then the network adapter, and second change the WEP encryption settings in the router and then the network adapter. Use the template in *Appendix A-5* to enter consistent values for SSID and WEP. After you apply either change to the router's settings, the computer will not be able to connect to the router until you make a similar change to its network adapter's settings.

If you get in trouble and you cannot configure the router, push the reset button on the router, and start all over again. Most routers have a **reset** button to restore it to the factory settings. Look for the reset button on the front or back panel of the router. Make sure that the router has power and then press and hold the reset button for about 10 seconds. The indicator lights on the router should flash and sequence a bit. After you complete the changes to these settings, your wireless router and your network should be functioning. Continue the configuration steps in *Section 10-3*.

Norton AntiVirus

This appendix describes how to use Norton AntiVirus to protect your computers from malicious software. Although the windows are a bit different from those displayed by McAfee VirusScan (see *Section 11-8*), the overall process is very similar.

 The windows and details we show are for the latest version of Norton AntiVirus. Your version of Norton AntiVirus may display slightly different windows.

J-1 Using Norton AntiVirus

You control Norton AntiVirus features and functions from its **System Status** window. This window also shows the date of the latest virus definition files. AntiVirus uses these files as a catalog of known viruses, Trojan horses, and worms. These files need updating frequently to ensure your copy of AntiVirus can protect you from newly discovered viruses, Trojan horses, and worms.

Figure J-1: Norton AntiVirus system tray icon

You bring up the **System Status** window by double-clicking on the Norton icon in the system tray (the lower right area of the screen). This window gives you a quick way to activate all the virus-scanning features.

Select the **Full System Scan** option. That will display the **Scan Now** button in the lower right corner. Click **Scan Now** to scan your entire computer for viruses.

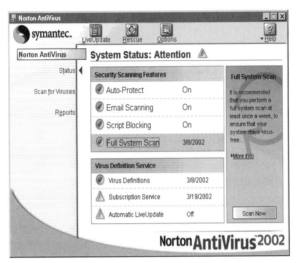

Figure J-2: System Status window

If AntiVirus detects an infected file, it displays a window with options to clean or delete the file. If AntiVirus cannot clean the file and you are not comfortable deleting files, you will need to seek professional help. When a scan is complete, AntiVirus displays the **Reports** window.

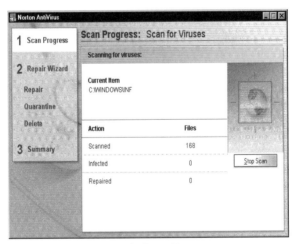

Figure J-3: Scan Progress

It gives a summary of the number of files scanned and any infected files.

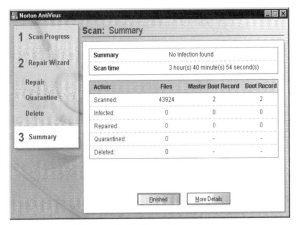

Figure J-4: Scan Summary

J-2 Updating your Norton Virus definition files

You download new and improved virus definition files over the Internet using the **LiveUpdate®** window (*Figure J-5*). You display this window by clicking on the **LiveUpdate** link in the **System Status** window (*Figure J-2*). Updating your virus definition file is critical when there is threat of a new virus. Norton usually charges a nominal fee for this service. **We strongly recommend that you subscribe to this service.** Just click **Next** to start the download process. When it completes, click **Finish** in the window that appears.

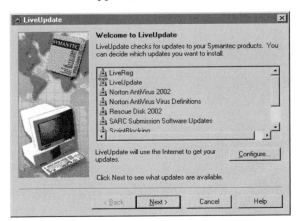

Figure J-5: LiveUpdate control window

J-3 Scanning an infected folder or file

If you suspect that a folder or a file contains a virus, you should scan the folder or file with AntiVirus. Right-click on the folder or file. In the menu, select **Scan With Norton AntiVirus**.

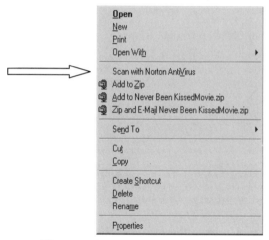

Figure J-6: Menu to select a scan of a file or folder

Norton AntiVirus scans the folder or file and produces a report similar to the one shown in *Figure J-7*.

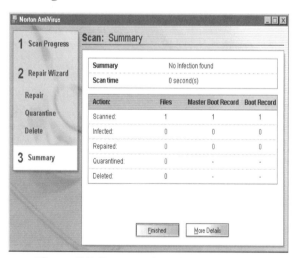

Figure J-7: Results of the file/folder scan

If the folder or file is infected and Norton AntiVirus can repair or delete the virus, you should allow it to do so. Otherwise, it is best to delete the folder or file and remove it from the Recycle Bin. Double-click **Recycle Bin** on your desktop and then click **Empty Recycle Bin**.

J-4 Enabling scanning for email

Email is now the most prevalent way of propagating viruses, Trojan horses, and worms. To increase your protection, you should enable scanning of both incoming and outgoing email messages.

If your email software behaves strangely or you see many messages in your outbox that you did not send, probably an email message infected your computer with a virus. If that is the case, we recommend that you close your email program and disconnect your computer from the network as quickly as possible. If your computer uses a wired connection, you should disconnect it by removing the blue RJ-45 Ethernet cable or the USB cable. If your computer uses a PC Card (PCMCIA) or USB network adapter, you should remove the card or device. If your computer connects using a wireless device, you need to disable the network adapter. Refer to *Appendix B-5*.

Some viruses take control of your computer and you cannot shut down your email program. Therefore, it is best to isolate the computer by eliminating its connection to the network. Then, you can take your time to identify and fix the problem before it contaminates other computers.

The windows below show how you can enable email scanning. The first window shows how to enable the **Email Scanning** option in the **System Status** window. By clicking on **Options**, you can specify that you want the scanning of both incoming and outgoing email.

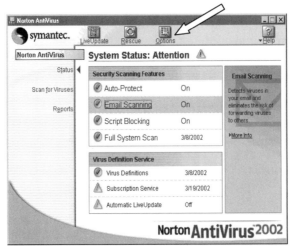

Figure J-8: Choosing Email Scanning

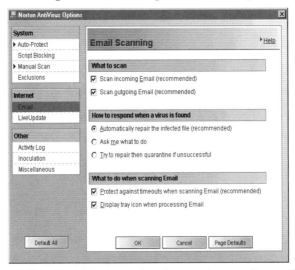

Figure J-9: Enabling incoming & outgoing email scanning

J-5 Conducting periodic scans

It is a good idea to scan your computer for viruses regularly. Follow the step in *Appendix J-1* to scan your entire computer manually. We recommend on-demand scans whenever you believe you have a virus in your computer but cannot pinpoint specifically which file or folder to scan.

In addition, Norton Antivirus provides a mechanism to schedule automatic periodic scans of your computer. It eliminates the guesswork and helps keep your computer free of viruses. First, click the **Schedule** button on the lower right corner of *Figure J-10*, a new window opens up with a **Schedule** tab (*Figure J-11*). From the drop-down menu choose weekly and the day and time of day that suites you. The default settings are weekly, on Friday's starting at 8:00 PM. Remember to click **OK** to accept the settings. We recommend that you scan your computer at least weekly.

Figure J-10: Scheduling automatic scans

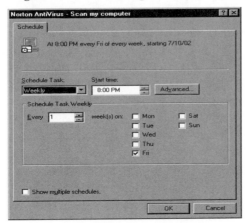

Figure J-11: Schedule weekly scans

Glossary

802.11b   The name of the industry standard that defines the current generation of 2.4GHz wireless data products.

address   The descriptive label of the location of an entity, such as a computer, a router, a home, or a business.

administrator   A user recognized by Windows as authorized to make changes to a computer's software and settings.

authentication   The process by which the identity of a principal in a transaction is established.

bandwidth   Describes the capacity of communications connections. Usually measured in "bits per second." High bandwidth is good.

broadband   Term used to describe a communications connection with bandwidth greater than 128 thousand bits per second. As opposed to narrowband.

BYOA   "Bring Your Own Access" (BYOA) is an option of AOL and MSN for reducing your monthly charge by reaching them using your Internet access instead of their dialup service.

CAT-5 or CAT-5E cable   A commonly used type of cable used to connect computers together. CAT-5 cable is a slightly older variety.

client computer   A computer that depends on another computer (called a server) for some service. For example, a computer that uses a shared printer located on another computer. A computer can be both a client and a server for different things.

computer name   The specific name you give to a computer to differentiate it from other computers, for example, BIGPC.

crossover RJ-45   (See also, Straight-through cable). A type
Ethernet cable   of cable sometimes used to connect network components together. We usually do not ask you to use this type of cable in your mini-internet.

decryption   The process of unscrambling an encrypted message.

default gateway   The address of the router or computer responsible for correctly routing a computer's IP packets.

DHCP   Dynamic Host Configuration Protocol (DHCP) is used to assign dynamic IP addresses and network settings. Used by your router to assign IP address to your computers.

domain name   Usually, the last two parts of an IP name, for example, "irs.gov." It describes a class of IP names assigned to a single authority (in this case, the IRS).

domain name   Name given to the Internet service that
service (DNS)   translates IP names to IP addresses.

DSL micro-filter   Devices that you connect to your phones and fax machines to separate them from your DSL data communications. If you do not install these on every phone and fax, your data communications may be interrupted.

dynamic IP address   An IP address that is only assigned to a computer temporarily. Compare to static IP address.

encryption   The process of scrambling data to make it difficult for intruders to interpret it.

encryption key   A secret password used to scramble or de-scramble data.

ESSID   Another name for SSID. The name that identifies a wireless network. In order to communicate with each other, wireless device must have the same SSID. Sometimes called network name.

Ethernet   The name of the data communication standard that applies mainly to LANs.

file server   Describes a computer that supports or offers files and folders to client computers. See client computer.

firewall   A device or a set of programs on a device that protects a LAN by using rules to control the flow of IP packets. Firewalls can either allow or refuse to pass each packet based on a set of rules.

gateway   See default gateway.

host name   The IP name of a computer.

HTTP   The Hypertext Transfer Protocol (HTTP) is the standard way web browsers communicate with websites.

HTTPS   Secure HTTP is the standard way
                       browsers communicate with websites
                       privately and securely. Usually used to
                       send private or personal information.

hub   A device that relays the same signals to
                       several connections. Serves the same
                       function as a switch.

infected file   A corrupted data file on a computer
                       usually containing a virus, Trojan horse,
                       or worm.

Internet   The public network of millions of routers
                       and computers that enable speedy
                       communication and information
                       exchange.

I/O   An abbreviation for input/output.

IP   Internet Protocol (IP) is the standard
                       manner that devices use to communicate
                       with each other on LANs and on the
                       Internet.

IP address   Internet Protocol (IP) address is a unique
                       identifier for a computer on the Internet.
                       Current IP addresses are of the form
                       123.123.123.123.

IP name   A unique name for a computer on the
                       Internet. Fully qualified IP names are of
                       the form www.irs.gov.

IP port   IP ports are numbers chosen by servers
                       and by your computer to identify each
                       separate "conversation" or application.
                       They are associated with every IP
                       address in each packet. Just as there are
                       source and destination IP addresses, there
                       are source and destination IP ports.

ISP   An Internet Service Provider (ISP)
                                 supplies Internet access to companies and
                                 customers. Usually, they also provide
                                 email services to users.

latency   The delay associated with sending a
                                 message or packet. Typically measured
                                 as the elapsed time from when a message
                                 is sent to when it is received. Low
                                 latency is good.

local area network   A collection of computers and network
(LAN)   elements sharing common network
                                 administration and infrastructure.
                                 Typically, a LAN is within a building or
                                 within a floor of a building.

mini-internet   The collection of computers, printers and
                                 other computer devices connected to
                                 each other using off-the-shelf and readily
                                 available network components. You can
                                 manage mini-internets and make them
                                 secure, and they easily connect to the big
                                 Internet through a single high-speed and
                                 shared connection.

modem   A device that converts computer
                                 messages to the form needed to transmit
                                 them over a communications link.

name   The generally agreed upon descriptive
                                 tag or label for computers, people,
                                 businesses or things.

narrowband   Term used to describe a communications
                                 connection with bandwidth less than 128
                                 thousand bits per second. As opposed to
                                 broadband.

network adapter

A device used to connect a computer to a network. For PCs, they come in three varieties: PCI, PC card (PCMCIA) and USB. They can be wired or wireless.

network address translation (NAT)

Specialized software running on a computer or a router that sits between your network and the Internet and protects the computers by hiding their IP address and IP ports.

packet

A unit of data (information) sent on the Internet. An Internet packet comprises a packet header and a packet body.

packet body

The portion of a packet that contains useful data. Sometimes referred to as "payload".

packet header

The portion of a packet that contains addressing and control information.

PC card (PCMCIA)

A credit card sized I/O or memory device, typically for notebook or laptop computers. PCMCIA stands for Personal Computer Memory Card International Association.

PCI card

Peripheral Component Interconnect (PCI) card is an input/output or video card that is installed inside a PC.

POP3

Post Office Protocol – version 3 (POP3) is the standard way an email client retrieves email messages from an email server.

PPPoE   Point to Point Protocol over Ethernet
                    (PPPoE) is the standard way DSL
                    providers allow a customer to pass name
                    and password to the provider and receive
                    a dynamic IP address and other network
                    settings.

print server   Describes a computer that supports or
                    offers print service to client computers.
                    See client computer.

private IP address   See also public IP address. One of a
                    special set of IP addresses that cannot be
                    used as IP address on the Internet. They
                    can be used on a mini-internet or LAN,
                    however. They are typically of the form
                    10.xxx.xxx.xxx or 192.168.xxx.xxx.

protocol   A standard way that devices, computers,
                    or applications use to communicate with
                    each other on LANs and on the Internet.

proxy   A computer program that sits between a
                    client computer and an Internet server. A
                    proxy examines the messages sent from
                    the client and either forwards them along,
                    or satisfies the request directly by using
                    locally stored information. Frequently
                    used by ISPs to improve performance of
                    web page requests.

public IP address   Any IP address that can be used on the
                    Internet to send and receive packets. See
                    private IP address.

RJ-11   A standard connector and jack type used
                    mainly for telephones and faxes.

RJ-45   A standard connector and jack type used
                    mainly by computers for connecting to a
                    LAN.

routable   A packet that can be delivered to the
                      addressed endpoint. Its IP address can be
                      used by Internet routers to determine
                      which router or computer to forward the
                      message to ensure delivery.

router   A network component, i.e. a special
                      purpose computer that correctly and
                      efficiently routes or passes Internet
                      packets.

server   A special purpose computer that provides
                      a service to other computers, e.g. a web
                      server.

share name   The name given to a shared resource on a
                      mini-internet. For example, share name
                      of a printer or a file.

shared printer   A printer that is shared on a mini-
                      internet. It is usually connected to a print
                      server, and accessed and used by client
                      computers.

SMTP   Simple Mail Transfer Protocol (SMTP) is
                      used to send email from your computer
                      to the mail server.

SSID   The name that identifies a wireless
                      network. In order to communicate with
                      each other, wireless devices in the same
                      network must have the same SSID.
                      Sometimes called ESSID or network
                      name.

SSL   Secure Sockets Layer is the way your
                      computer and an Internet server
                      handshake, agree on a secret key, and
                      communicate securely.

static IP address	A permanent IP address assigned to you by your service provider. This IP address is your Wide Area Network (WAN) IP address, and each computer on the Internet uses it to talk to your computers
straight through Ethernet cable	An Ethernet cable that is used to connect network components within the LAN.
subnet mask	Information that allows the various Internet routers to direct packets to and from you.
switch	A network device that connects network devices (e.g., computers, routers, switches) to each other. Switches replicate the packets they receive from one device and make them available to the other devices.
TCP/IP	Transmission Control Protocol/Internet Protocol, is the way that computers and network devices send and receive packets to their intended destination with a high-level assurance of correct delivery.
top level domains	The highest-level grouping of Internet names, for example, `.com`, `.gov`, `.org`, `.net`, and `.uk` that describe networks of companies, government agencies, non-profit organizations, network providers, and countries.
URL	Universal Resource Locator. The Internet name given to items you can reference from your browser. For example, the URL for a web page might be `http://www.irs.gov`.

USB   Universal Serial Bus (USB) is the name
                           given to a simple and widely used
                           method of connecting devices to
                           computers. An advantage of USB
                           devices is that they usually can be
                           connected and removed while computers
                           are running.

WEP   Wired Equivalent Privacy (WEP) is the
                           standard way wireless devices encrypt
                           data for privacy and security.

wide area network   A computer network that covers a wide
(WAN)   geographic region or area, such as a city,
                           state, or country.

wired   Computers, devices, and networks that
                           use wires or cables to connect.

wireless   Computers, devices, and networks that
                           connect by using radio technology
                           instead of wires or cables. For example,
                           802.11b is one wireless technology.

wizard   A software application that simplifies the
                           tasks of configuring devices and settings
                           in computers and routers.

workgroup   A group of computers set up to share
                           printers, files, and other devices in the
                           Windows operating environment.

WWW   The World Wide Web (WWW) is the
                           collection of computer servers you can
                           easily access on the Internet from your
                           browser.

Index

HRATOM, LLC. Reader Response Form

Title of this book:	Networks in a Flash Making Broadband Work for You
Rating of this book:	☐ Very Good ☐ Good ☐ Satisfactory ☐ Fair ☐ Poor

Where I got this book:	☐ Bookstore:
	☐ Website:
	☐ Service provider:
	☐ Equipment provider:

What I liked about this book:

What needs to be changed:

Comments:

Version of Windows I'm using:	☐ XP ☐ 2000 ☐ ME ☐ 98 ☐ Other

Name:

Company:

Address:

City/State/Zip:

Please send completed form to: (or email comments to editor@BooksInAFlash.com)	HRATOM, LLC P.O. Box 4426 Mountain View, CA 94040-0426